KILL ME NOW

T0314750

BRAD FRASER

KILL ME NOW

OBERON BOOKS
LONDON

WWW.OBERONBOOKS.COM

First published in 2015 by Oberon Books Ltd
521 Caledonian Road, London N7 9RH
Tel: +44 (0) 20 7607 3637 / Fax: +44 (0) 20 7607 3629
e-mail: info@oberonbooks.com
www.oberonbooks.com

A catalogue record for this book is available from the British
Library.

PB ISBN: 9781783198092
E ISBN: 9781783198757

Cover design by AKA
Photography by Hugo Glendinning

Visit www.oberonbooks.com to read more about all our books
and to buy them. You will also find features, author interviews and
news of any author events, and you can sign up for e-newsletters
so that you're always first to hear about our new releases.

For Alex. For Rudy and John

On Characters and Casting

BY BRAD FRASER

I am a queer Metis person from a rough background. I grew up in roadside motels in northern B.C. and attended a dizzying array of schools in my early years. The people I encountered during that time, and throughout my life, were young and old, good and bad, short and tall. They were able-bodied and disabled. They were male and female and trans, straight, gay, and queer, bi and asexual. Some were even straight, middle-class and white, the group I least related to. They were my family, my friends, and the citizens of the many towns we passed through. And, like me, many of them were outsiders in some way.

I am a writer. I tell the stories of these people. Outsider stories. Our stories. Not once did it occur to me to ask if I had a "right" to portray these people. Portraying people is what writers do. I chose to write for the theatre not only because of my love of the form but because it has always been the place where those who live on the margins of society are first able to share and find their voice.

In the context of my background and experience, I'm baffled by the judgmental tenor of the current controversy over physically-abled actors playing physically challenged characters. Not that we shouldn't be having this discussion – of course we should – but let's do it in a nuanced and pragmatic way.

Physical disability is a very broad spectrum. Each individual manifestation of disability has its own attributes. Theatre also has almost infinite variety. Each production has its own requirements. Each character has its own demands.

In the theatre, unlike the electronic media, an actor's job is not just to act, but also to control the flow and pace of the play. What is seen onstage is only the tip of a much larger backstage iceberg of fast-paced manoeuvring that involves racing around in the dark, lightning-quick changes, and often a great deal of physical and mental dexterity. Actors, whether able-bodied or challenged, have to rise to these challenges, or the production will fail.

This is not to suggest that disabled actors can't do theatre, but that the way in which it is done will vary greatly by individual and role, and, in the commercial theatre at least, this will always come down to a question of time and money.

Acting is one of the hardest professions in the world. Most of those in the business will know far more rejection than success. It doesn't matter if you look the part, you've lived the part, or you are the part – the director and producers will go with whoever they think will lead to highest ticket sales, and ninety-nine percent of the time the actor hired will not be you, regardless of race, gender, sex or physical capability. Rejection, for actors, is an equal opportunity experience.

Equating able-bodied actors playing physically challenged characters with historic blackface is a false equivalence. Disability, like queerness, is potentially found in everyone regardless of race or gender. Further complicating the issue, disability, like race and gender, is a mutable and evolving thing. Advanced prosthetics let people who were once considered disabled outperform the average able-bodied person. Intermarriage and the mixing of the races increasingly makes race and skin colour a more complicated issue. Gender is also fluid. Men can become women, women can become men and those who choose not to identify as either are fighting for their own recognition.

Can Othello only be played by someone who had two black parents? What if one parent was of another background? Just how black does Othello have to be? Conversely, it is equally valid to ask if Willy Loman has to have both of his hands, or if he has to be able to walk without an aid, if he has to be able to see or even if he has to be white. Can the lead dancer in the chorus of the latest mega-musical lead the troupe on advanced prosthetics rather than legs? How does a director communicate ideas to a deaf and mute actress who is playing Helen Keller? How versatile does the actor need to be in a single show; will they be playing multiple characters and how will that work? What if the character is only differently-abled for part of the narrative? Can a disabled actor play the able-bodied part as convincingly as an able-bodied actor can portray the disability? If Joey in *Kill Me Now* should only be played by an actor with a true physical challenge, then must the actor playing Jake also suffer from spinal stenosis?

The answers to these questions can only be found in the context of each individual production, process and performer, not in endless reductive comments in the corporate press and social media. They'll only be found when the theatre truly opens itself up to the possibility of actors with physical disabilities playing parts where their physical ability is irrelevant or interpretational. Casting is all about context.

As for those who complain that plays like *Kill Me Now* don't reflect the specific truth of their own experience with life or disability, and who denigrate the authenticity of challenging dramatic narratives that don't tell the stories of their own less tragic lives, I would remind them that theatre is drama, drama needs conflict, and there aren't a lot of successful plays about families who live conflict free and carry on cheerfully despite difficulties. Criticizing my work for its dramatic failings is fair game, but criticizing it because it doesn't tell the story of your particular personal experience speaks to a lack of understanding of how plays work and what they're for, and, frankly, a rather telling narcissism. All dramatic characters are metaphorical constructs that serve the needs of a story. All artists work with their imaginations. To ask anyone to limit that imagination for political purposes seems to me the worst kind of oppression of all.

In the end, this is an important and necessary discussion, and one that I believe will eventually lead to positive change. But as we engage these issues let's keep in mind that there is no blanket solution or easy answer. Solutions will only be found by considering specific performers in specific productions, not with the sweeping imposition of universal policies.

Context. It's everything.

Characters

JAKE STURDY
Late thirties to early-forties.

JOEY STURDY
Seventeen. Born with an extra chromosome
which he is severely disabled by, particularly his
hands which he can poke with but not grasp.

TWYLA STURDY
Early-thirties.

ROBYN DARTONA
Forties.

ROWDY AKERS
Eighteen. Rowdy is affected by Fetal Alcohol
Syndrome as well as other issues.

The Setting

*The Sturdy home including Joey's very specifically
appointed bathroom and other places.*

Kill Me Now premiered at Workshop West Playwright's Theatre, Edmonton, Alberta, Canada, on September 9, 2013.

The first European performance of *Kill Me Now* took place on Thursday 19 February 2015 at Park Theatre, London.

DARKNESS. THE SOUND OF WATER RUNNING. LIGHTS RISE ON A LARGE TUB FILLED WITH WATER. JAKE IS BATHING JOEY.

JAKE: Not too hot?

JOEY: Nuh. (No.)

JAKE: You're sure?

JOEY: Yuh!

JAKE: Deep enough?

JOEY: Yuh.

JAKE: Okay then.

          JAKE TURNS THE WATER OFF.

JAKE: Soap. Shampoo. Wash cloth.

JOEY: Nuh sampuh. (No shampoo.)

JAKE: Okay. It's clean enough. How was school?

JOEY: Nukuh (Okay.)

JAKE: Did you get into any trouble?

JOEY: Nuh.

JAKE: You didn't push Daisy?

JOEY: See spih uh muh. (She spit on me.)

JAKE: Why?

JOEY: Ah nuh nuh. (I don't know.)

JAKE: Joey.

JOEY: See uh how. (She's a whore.)

JAKE: Joey!

JOEY: See sah ah hungy. (She said I'm ugly.)

JAKE: Why would she say that?

JOEY: See uh how.

JAKE: Buddy please.

JOEY: Ah guh mah. (I get mad.)

JAKE: You have to be careful Joey. You're too big to get mad like that. It scares people.

JOEY: Ah hungy.

JAKE: No.

JOEY: Flee. (Freak.)

JAKE: You're a nice guy. You have to let people see that. Especially the girls.

JOEY: Noh Dezzy see fah ad soopuh. (Not Daisy she's fat and stupid.)

JAKE: What people say doesn't matter. You know that.

JOEY: Muh buh hud. (My butt hurts.)

JAKE: Have you been wiping it properly?

JOEY: Ah tah. (I try.)

JAKE: I'll put some cream on it after we wash.

JOEY: Sanks. (Thanks.)

JAKE: Remember get as much toilet paper around your fingers as you can.

JOEY: Ah cand gid id owv avda. (I can't get it off after.)

JAKE: Then get Phillip to do it. He's at school to help you.

JOEY: Ah duh luh kih. (I don't like it.)

JAKE: You're okay with me doing it.

JOEY: Yuh muh dah. (You're my dad.)

JAKE: Yes I am.

JOEY: Ooh duh thik ah hungy. (You don't think I'm ugly.)

JAKE: I think you're a very handsome boy.

JOEY: Yuh shih. (You're sick.)

JAKE: I am. Hold still so I can clean your ears.

JOEY: Dah!

JAKE RINSES JOEY.

JAKE: That's not so bad. Hold on just a bit more there.

JOEY: Kehn. (Clean.)

JAKE: Yes and – uh – excited.

JOEY: Bonuh. (Boner.)

JAKE: Yeah.

JOEY: Suruh. (Sorry.)

JAKE: No it's – don't worry. Completely natural at your age.

JOEY: Ah nuh seshulah matuh. (I'm now sexually mature.)

JAKE: They go away.

JOEY: Wun sin ah wah. (Once in a while.)

JAKE: The services might be able to send someone to help with that.

JOEY: Weewee? (Really?)

JAKE: There are professionals who do that sort of thing.

JOEY: Nuh.

JAKE: You're sure? Some of them are very pretty.

JOEY: Nuwuh wunuh luh ah muh. (No one wants to look at me.)

JAKE: There are also machines they can use –

JOEY: Mushuh? (Machines?)

JAKE: Apparently. I'm not quite sure how they work –

JOEY: Uh duh wun sub muchuh uh muh dig. (I don't want some machine on my dick.)

JAKE: You can't rub it against anything or something like that?

JOEY: Nuh. Un muh hunsh – (No. And my hands –)

JAKE: Maybe this will help.

JAKE SPRAYS JOEY DOWN WITH COLD WATER. JOEY SCREAMS IN SHOCK, LAUGHING.

JOEY: Dah. Staw. Staw! (Dad. Stop. Stop!)

JAKE: It isn't that cold.

JOEY: Yuh mun. (You're mean.)

JAKE: Made your boner go away.

JOEY: Yuh.

JAKE: Good.

JAKE GETS JOEY OUT OF THE WATER. JAKE DRIES JOEY OFF.

JAKE: Okay?

JOEY: Fuh. (Fine.)

JAKE: Hold still.

JOEY: Huhuh ub. (Hurry up.)

JAKE: You alright?

JOEY: Fuh. (Fine.)

JAKE: Let's dry you off.

JOEY: Nuso har. (Not so hard.)

JAKE GETS A CREAM HE SPREADS ON JOEY'S ASS.

JAKE: Hold on.

JOEY: Ih coh. (It's cold.)

JAKE: It'll help that rash.

JOEY: Ukuh. (Okay.)

JAKE: Does it feel better?

JOEY: Yuh.

JAKE: Into your underpants.

JOEY: Nuh deepah. (No diaper.)

JAKE: Until you can wipe your own ass properly you're going to have to wear them bud. This isn't a debate.

JOEY SULLENLY ALLOWS HIS FATHER TO HELP HIM INTO THE UNDERWEAR.

JOEY: Deepah.

JAKE: Safety pants.

JOEY: Ah nuh nee fuhin sayve panz! (I don't need fucking safety pants!)

JAKE: Watch your language.

JOEY: Yuh wuhuvuh. (Yeah whatever.)

JAKE: I mean it

JOEY: Ruh. (Right.)

JAKE DRESSES HIM.

JAKE: I'm not the enemy. You just tell me what you need and I'll do whatever I can to make it happen. You know that.

JOEY: Yuh.

JAKE: And if it's just general adolescent angst and I'm the easiest target then I'd suggest finding someplace more constructive to direct it because I don't deserve it.

JOEY IS NOW DRESSED. JAKE HELPS HIM INTO HIS WHEELCHAIR.

JOEY: Duh ooh kish muhmuh. (Did you kiss mommy.)

JAKE: Of course. You kiss people when you love them. It's natural.

JOEY: Nuh guh wuh kish muh. (No girl will kiss me.)

JAKE: Someone will.

JOEY: Nuh. Ah hungy.

JAKE: You're a fine looking boy.

JOEY: Dun lah tuh muh. (Don't lie to me.)

            TWYLA IS HEARD FROM OFFSTAGE.

TWYLA: Hey?

JAKE: We're in the bathroom.

TWYLA: Are you naked?

JAKE: Not anymore.

            TWYLA ENTERS CARRYING HER BAG AND A PLAINLY WRAPPED BOX.

TWYLA: Good.

JOEY: Eh Un Tuhluh. (Hey Aunt Twyla.)

TWYLA: Hey brat.

JAKE: Hey.

TWYLA: You boys all cleaned up?

JOEY: Yuh. Kehn.

JAKE: He had some drama at school today.

TWYLA: What's pissing you off?

JAKE: He pushed Daisy.

TWYLA: Don't be pushing people.

JOEY: See sud ah wuh – (She said I was…)

TWYLA: You are too big to be pushing anyone around.

JAKE: You are.

TWYLA: Especially girls. I want it to stop. Seriously.

            PAUSE.

TWYLA: I mean it.

JOEY: Uhkuh. (Okay.)

            PAUSE.

TWYLA: You're looking hot in that shirt.

JAKE: He picked it out himself.

JOEY: Feez nush. (Feels nice.)

JAKE: How's that swarthy guy?

TWYLA: Hector. Fine. Don't ask.

JOEY: Wus ih duh bosh? (What's in the box?)

TWYLA: Wouldn't you like to know?

JOEY: Ish id fuh muh? (Is it for me?)

TWYLA: Why do you think everything's for you?

JOEY: Cuh uh spuhshuh. (Because I'm special.)

TWYLA: This is true.

JOEY: Wuh hiz ih? (What is it?)

> *SHE GIVES HIM THE PACKAGE. HE IMMEDIATELY BANGS ON IT HARD.*

TWYLA: Joey no!

JOEY: Suruh. (Sorry.)

TWYLA: Don't wanna break it.

JAKE: What is it?

TWYLA: Ready to open it?

JOEY: Yuh.

TWYLA: Want me to do it or dad?

JOEY: Ooh. (You.)

> *SHE TAKES THE PACKAGE FROM HIM.*

TWYLA: Hold your breath buddy boy because it is a brand spanking new – *(SHE TEARS THE WRAPPING OFF OF THE BOX AND OPENS IT.)* – state of the art computer tablet!

JOEY: Poodah tabuh? (Computer tablet?)

TWYLA: Yeah. Check it out – multi-media capabilities a
           writing program mail camera –

JAKE: That's a lot of buttons. You know his motor control
           and touch ability aren't really –

           TWYLA TURNS THE TABLET ON.

TWYLA: I talked to the programmer before I bought it and
           he customized it for us. Basically there are three
           buttons he needs to hit on the touch screen and
           they're big. Just poke or slide. It's even got a phone.

JOEY: Uh foe? (A phone?)

TWYLA: Watch this.

           SHE HITS A BUTTON ON HER COMMUNICATIONS DEVICE.
           HIS PAD BEEPS.

JOEY: Cuh. (Cool.)

TWYLA: Answer it.

           JOEY HITS A BUTTON.

JOEY: Ah suh yuh. (I see you.)

TWYLA: *(INTO HER DEVICE.)* And I can see you.

JOEY: Fuh yuh. (Fuck yeah.)

JAKE: Joey.

JOEY: Suruh. (Sorry.)

TWYLA: I tied him into your net connection – full access
           including real time visual chat synchronized with
           your phone.

JAKE: Wow.

TWYLA: Aren't you glad I'm ten years younger than you?

JAKE: Totally. I could never do that shit.

JOEY: *(FASCINATED WITH TABLET.)* Gumsh? (Games?)

TWYLA: Just hit the button marked games.

JOEY: Gumsh?

TWYLA: You know how to spell it.

JOEY: Gumsh!

            *HE HITS A BUTTON AND THERE'S A NOISE FROM THE
            MACHINE.*

TWYLA: Not so hard. You have to be careful. Now pick
            something from the menu.

JAKE: Something without shooting.

JOEY: Wuh? (Why?)

JAKE: Because you get too aggressive.

TWYLA: I had them delete the aggression games. Try the
            Magic Worms. Play around. You'll figure out what
            works best for you real fast.

JAKE: Thank your Aunt.

JOEY: *(DISMISSIVELY.)* Sankoo. (Thank you.)

TWYLA: You're welcome.

JAKE: You're too good to us. I could never afford –

TWYLA: Don't sweat it. I got the staff discount.

JAKE: He's all cleaned up. Just brush his teeth before bed.

TWYLA: He'll be okay with that?

JAKE: Why wouldn't he?

TWYLA: He seems to be getting a bit – shy around me these
            days.

JAKE: Yeah. Puberty finally hit.

TWYLA: He doesn't want his aunt wiping his ass or washing
            his feet anymore.

JAKE: He's embarrassed.

TWYLA: I've taken care of him since he was a kid.

JAKE: You're still a woman.

TWYLA: I get it.

JAKE: His melatonin and night medications are where
          they always are.

TWYLA: He'll have his face in that tablet all night.

JAKE: What are you going to do?

TWYLA: I've got a new book and some messages to answer.

JAKE: The swarthy guy's not coming over?

TWYLA: Go to your hockey game.

JAKE: My cell's on if you need me.

TWYLA: We'll be fine.

          *JAKE EXITS. TWYLA MOVES TO JOEY AND WATCHES HIM
          PLAYING WITH THE TABLET.*

TWYLA: You like it?

          JOEY NODS, IGNORING HER.

TWYLA: It can speak for you too. Just type in what you want
          to say.

          JOEY NODS.

TWYLA: Let me show you –

          JOEY PUSHES HER HAND AWAY.

JOEY: Um ukuh Un Twuhluh. (I'm okay Aunt Twyla.)

TWYLA: Okay. Ignore me then.

JOEY: Yuh.

          *LIGHTS RISE ON A SMALL APARTMENT. ROBYN IS IN THE
          PROCESS OF TIDYING UP. TO ONE SIDE IS A MESSED
          UP FOLD-OUT BED. SHE WEARS HER SLIP, BRA ETC.
          HER OTHER CLOTHES ARE LAID ON A CHAIR NEXT TO
          SOME MALE CLOTHING. A SHOWER IS HEARD OFF. THE
          SHOWER STOPS.*

ROBYN: It's ten to.

JAKE: These love handles are becoming jelly rolls.

JAKE ENTERS FROM THE BATHROOM IN HIS BOXER SHORTS. HE'S DRYING HIS HAIR ETC.

ROBYN: You look just fine.

JAKE: *(KISSES HER.)* So do you.

THEY DRESS AS THEY SPEAK.

JAKE: Did we finish quicker than usual?

ROBYN: The event was somewhat – truncated.

JAKE: Really? I didn't even –

ROBYN: You're distracted.

JAKE: You didn't come.

ROBYN: Don't worry.

JAKE: You know I feel like a failure if I don't get you off.

ROBYN: Stop –

JAKE: Seriously.

ROBYN: Twelve years and the times I haven't gotten off I can count on one hand. Relax.

JAKE: I guess I just –

ROBYN: What?

JAKE: Joey got an erection when I was bathing him today.

ROBYN: Most teenage boys get an erection touching mud. I don't think you should take it personally.

JAKE: For a while it looked like he wouldn't mature sexually at all.

ROBYN: So it's a good thing.

JAKE: It's just one more thing he knows he can't do normally.

ROBYN: Right.

JAKE: When I was a kid extra chromosomes and unexplained bone mutations gave you super powers not crippling disabilities.

ROBYN Ha.

JAKE FOLDS THE BEDDING.

JAKE: How's Howard?

ROBYN: A bit depressed. He has been ever since Teddy got married.

JAKE: Does he ever inquire about – these nights away?

ROBYN: He's less interested in my bridge club than I am in his quarterly visits to Vegas.

JAKE: My family still buys the hockey thing. Even with the shape I'm in –

ROBYN: Have you written anything?

JAKE: I spend an hour in front of the keyboard every night after marking submissions but I just don't have the – energy to sustain that kind of concentration. I wish I had the money to rent us a small place somewhere.

ROBYN: Anastasia's pottery class works out well for everyone. And don't worry about Joey.

JAKE: No?

ROBYN: He's still a teenage boy whatever his challenges. I raised two of them and it's all about erections and crusty bed sheets. Very soon he'll insist everything you say is wrong and you'll spend three years feeling like the stupidest person in the world. You can't take it personally.

JAKE: I know. It's just – he's figuring out that there are no women who'd want him and that's – it's not fair.

ROBYN: It's not. I'm sorry. Anastasia will be back any second.

JAKE: Thank you.

JAKE KISSES HER QUICKLY AND EXITS. LIGHTS RISE ON TWYLA IN JAKE'S LIVING ROOM WATCHING SOMETHING ON TELEVISION WHILE ENJOYING A DRINK. JAKE ENTERS.

JAKE: Any drama?

TWYLA: He made a bit of a fuss when I took the computer away but he's out now.

JAKE: Great.

TWYLA: Who won?

JAKE: I did.

TWYLA: You know if there's another night you want to go out I'll watch him.

JAKE: You do too much already.

TWYLA: You need to get more exercise.

JAKE: Hefting Joey around keeps me in shape.

TWYLA: The Services will send people to help.

JAKE: The Services are way more interested in monitoring my income to make sure I'm not "beating the system" than they are in helping us.

TWYLA: There's no shame in letting someone else take care of your special needs son from time to time.

JAKE: He gets agitated if I'm away for too long.

TWYLA: No he doesn't. Jake – Viola and mom have been dead for fifteen years.

JAKE: What's your point?

TWYLA: It wouldn't kill you to develop a life.

JAKE: Twyla –

TWYLA: You're not going to be around forever.

JAKE: Neither is he.

TWYLA: We don't know that. His condition is so rare. He could outlive all of us.

PAUSE.

JAKE: You're sure you're okay to drive? The guest room's –

TWYLA: Whatever happened to those guys you used to pal around with? Attila and Chucky and that other guy? Whatsisname?

JAKE: Sandro. That was high school. I haven't seen them in decades.

TWYLA: You should call them. Get together.

JAKE: I wouldn't even know what to say.

TWYLA: Invite them over here.

JAKE: And what – have them piss over the top of Joey's reinforced toilet seat the way I do? Hope they look past the stains in the linoleum? The adult disposable diaper bin? No one wants to visit here.

TWYLA: Then go out.

JAKE: I don't see that happening.

TWYLA: What about writing another book?

JAKE: Do you want me to walk you to the car?

TWYLA: No I'm fine. Good night.

JAKE: Thanx sis.

TWYLA EXITS. A LIGHT RISES ON JOEY AND ROWDY IN THE LIVING ROOM PLAYING ON THE TABLET.

ROWDY: Okay now shoot the marine in the head and gun the engine.

JOEY: Nuh? (Now?)

ROWDY: Right now.

JOEY BANGS AT THE COMPUTER QUICKLY

ROWDY: Great. Now run that hooker down and hit the old lady with the baby carriage.

JOEY: Goh ih. (Got it.)

ROWDY: Now go left. Left stupid!

JOEY: Sih. (Shit.)

ROWDY: I told you left.

JOEY: Uh duh. (I died.)

ROWDY: Sick game huh?

JOEY: Yuh. Ah gunuh puh uguh un kih thah guh. (Yeah. I'm gonna play again and kill that guy.)

ROWDY: In the next stage the marines become these roid monsters and you get a chainsaw.

JOEY: Cuh. (Cool.)

ROWDY TAKES THE TABLET FROM JOEY.

ROWDY: This is a great thing.

JOEY: Gih ih bug. (Give it back.)

ROWDY: Relax. I'm checking it out.

JOEY: Wowdee!

ROWDY: There's lotsa porn on here eh. Anything you can imagine and a buncha shit you can't –

JOEY HITS ROWDY.

JOEY: Gih ih bag. (Give it back.)

ROWDY: Don't fucking hit me.

JOEY: Ih muh! (It's mine!)

ROWDY TOSSES THE TABLE ONTO JOEY'S CHAIR.

ROWDY: Now quit whining.

TWYLA ENTERS.

TWYLA: Hello.

JOEY: Huh Un Tuhluh. (Hi Aunt Twyla.)

TWYLA: Where's Jake?

ROWDY: Had to run out.

TWYLA: Who are you?

JOEY: Wowdee. (Rowdy.)

TWYLA: Your friend from school.

ROWDY: Rowdy Akers. *(MOVES TO TWYLA AND SHAKES HER HAND AGGRESIVELY.)* Nice to finally meet you Aunt Twyla.

TWYLA: Twyla's fine. Jake left you to look after Joey?

ROWDY: I might be a bit retarded but I'm not stupid. It's mostly fetal alcohol syndrome eh. Joey never said you were so hot.

TWYLA: Could you please not stand quite so close to me.

ROWDY: Am I crowding your personal space? I do that sometimes.

TWYLA: No I prefer nose to nose contact on a first meeting.

ROWDY: That's – um – it's sharkism right?

TWYLA: What?

ROWDY: Sharkism. When you say something in a bitchy way but you mean the opposite.

TWYLA: Sarcasm?

ROWDY: Right.

TWYLA: Yes. It is.

ROWDY: Sorry. I guess I'm just a little messed up cuz you're so hot and everything.

TWYLA: Please stop saying that.

ROWDY: But I mean it –

JOEY: Wowdee!

ROWDY: What? I'm being polite. That's what you do when you meet girls Joe.

JOEY: Suh muh Un. (She's my Aunt.)

ROWDY: I have a really big dick.

TWYLA: That's your idea of polite?

ROWDY: A lot of ladies go for it.

JOEY: Ih weewee bih. (It's really big.)

TWYLA: I didn't come here to find out how big anyone's penis is okay thank you?

ROWDY: Am I being inappropriate?

TWYLA: Yes.

ROWDY: You mad?

TWYLA: No.

ROWDY: You seem pissed.

JOEY: Shush luh thuh. (She's like that.)

JAKE ENTERS.

JAKE: Hey.

TWYLA: Hi.

JOEY: Duh wuh kik. (That was quick.)

JAKE: I just ran to the courier on the corner.

TWYLA: I've met Rowdy.

JAKE: Your paths have never crossed before?

TWYLA: He offered to show me his penis.

JAKE: *(TO ROWDY.)* We talked about that.

ROWDY: I know.

JAKE: If people want to see your penis they'll ask.

ROWDY: But –

JOEY: Wowdee les guh tuh muh ruh. (Rowdy let's go to
           my room.)

TWYLA: Good to meet you.

ROWDY: Good idea. Nice to meet you Twyla.

           *ROWDY SHAKES HER HAND FIRMLY. HE MOVES TO JAKE
           AND SHAKES HIS HAND.*

ROWDY: Good to see you Mr Sturdy.

           ROWDY AND JOEY EXIT.

TWYLA: Does he shake everyone's hand?

JAKE: Every time. He's been very protective of my boy for
           some reason.

TWYLA: Well there's that.

JAKE: Would you like me to ask him to leave?

TWYLA: It's okay. How is it I haven't met him before?

JAKE: I tend to have him over on the days you can't help
           out.

TWYLA: Right.

JAKE: Okay then I'm gonna –

TWYLA: Jake where do you play hockey?

JAKE: You know – at different arenas.

TWYLA: Where?

JAKE: In the – suburbs.

TWYLA: And you never practice or anything? You just play a
           full out game of hockey every Tuesday night?

JAKE: Just old guys farting around.

TWYLA: Right. Good luck.

JAKE: Thanks.

           *JAKE EXITS. LIGHTS RISE ON JOEY AND ROWDY IN JOEY'S
           ROOM. THEY'RE ON THE TABLET.*

ROWDY: Those're some hot babes eh?

JOEY: Tohtuluh. (Totally.)

ROWDY: Sorry I ain't been by in a while. Shit gets busy right.

JOEY: Suh. (Sure.)

ROWDY: That fat snatch at the group home wants to know where I am every fucking minute of every fucking day.

JOEY: Duh yuh fun ah jaw yuh? (Did you find a job yet?)

ROWDY: I think so. They're looking for someone to clean and shit at the chicken place and the guy who interviewed me was real interested. I bet I get it.

JOEY: Gwed. (Great.)

ROWDY: I keep applying with the city to work in parks and shit – but they never call me in for an interview.

JOEY: Day shug. (They suck.)

ROWDY: I need some dough. That allowance from the Services is nothing. You wanna blow a fattie?

JOEY: Yuh.

ROWDY LIGHTS A JOINT THEY SHARE IT WITH ROWDY HOLDING IT TO JOEY'S LIPS WHEN IT'S HIS TURN TO SMOKE.

ROWDY: You talk to your old man about our idea?

JOEY: Nuh.

ROWDY: Why not?

JOEY: Ah nunuh. Duh tum huznuh bun ruh. (I don't know. The time hasn't been right.)

ROWDY: You're eighteen next year right?

JOEY: Yuh.

ROWDY: And I'm nearly twenty-one. Try not to drool on my finger bud.

JOEY: Suruh. Ah huva luh mah duh nuh. (Sorry. I have to let my dad know.)

ROWDY: Sure yeah. Your dad's the best. But you and me would be a good match sharing a place eh? The government gives us both money for being gimped out and the services do everything we can't. No one telling us what to do.

JOEY: Yuh.

ROWDY: He's not gonna like it but if you bring it up now it'll make it easier later.

JOEY: Subuh. (Subtle.)

ROWDY: Exactly. You're so smart. We'll get some apartment on the east side where people like us live. I'll bring home all the pussy I want. I'll bring you some too.

JOEY: Nuh pussuh wansh muh. (No pussy wants me.)

ROWDY: There's a pussy for everybody bro.

JOEY: Ah hungy.

ROWDY: I'll let you watch.

JOEY: Duh buh suh fuguh goes. (Don't be so fucking gross.)

ROWDY: Well you like watching them on the net right?

JOEY: Yuh buh… (Yeah but…)

ROWDY: What?

JOEY: Dun muh fuh uf muh. (Don't make fun of me.)

ROWDY: Hey what? Me?

JOEY: Ah cand. (I can't.)

ROWDY: Can't what?

JOEY: Jag ih. (Jack it.)

ROWDY: Shit fuck dude that's kinda like being crippled.

JOEY: Ah nuh. (I know.)

ROWDY: Don't sweat it. I'll find some chick to suck you off.

JOEY: Ah tuh hungy. (I'm too ugly.)

ROWDY: I'll get a blind chick. Or turn out the light. Yeah.
           That's probably easier than finding a blind hooker.

JOEY: Thuhlul seel fee huh tiseted ah mah. (They'll still
           feel how twisted I am.)

ROWDY: So hey Joe you aren't telling me this to get me to
           play with your cock or anything like that are you?

JOEY: Sob! Yuh benuh soopuh. (Stop. You're being stupid.)

ROWDY: I know. Sorry bud. It's just I'm not you know.

JOEY: Muh udduh. (Me either.)

ROWDY: I bet there's someone at The Services who jacks off
           sexually frustrated retards.

JOEY: Yuh bud hihut buh suwuh fah. (Yeah but it'd be
           someone fat.)

ROWDY: *(LAUGHS.)* Or really old.

JOEY: Uh hungy!

ROWDY: With one of those big moles with hairs sticking out
           of it!

JOEY: Oh dah tits. (On their tits.)

           THEY BOTH LAUGH. IT TRAILS OFF

ROWDY: Did we smoke that joint?

JOEY: Uh yuh. (Oh yeah.)

ROWDY: Gimme your pad. You won't believe what summa
           these broads will do for money –

JOEY: *(HANDING HIM THE PAD.)* Ukuh. (Okay.)

           TWYLA IS HEARD OFF.

TWYLA: Joey!

JOEY: Wuh?

TWYLA: I can smell the weed.

JOEY: Guh why. (Go away.)

TWYLA: Let me in. Joey.

ROWDY: Come in.

           ROWDY OPENS THE DOOR. TWYLA ENTERS.

TWYLA: Do you have any idea how marijuana might react
           with his other medications?

ROWDY: Uh yeah – I've been smoking him up since he was
           like twelve.

JOEY: Ah fah. (I'm fine.)

ROWDY: I've got another spliff if you're –

TWYLA: Rowdy I think maybe it's time for you to go home.

ROWDY: You throwing me out?

TWYLA: It's time for Joey's supper.

JOEY: Muh fuduh. (My feeding.)

ROWDY: Like in the zoo.

JOEY: Zacluh. (Exactly.)

ROWDY: Like a fucking hippo man.

JOEY: Oh uh muhkuh. (Or a monkey!)

           THEY LAUGH.

TWYLA: Stoned teenagers. Very amusing. Have a nice night.

ROWDY: Lighten up mam. Life's short.

           ROWDY GIVES JOEY A HUG.

ROWDY: Stay outa trouble.

JOEY: Yuh tuh. (You too.)

           ROWDY MOVES TO TWYLA AND HOLDS HIS HAND OUT.

ROWDY: Charmed to meet you.

SHE SHAKES HIS HAND RELUCTANTLY.

TWYLA: Likewise.

ROWDY EXITS.

TWYLA: Are you ready to eat?

JOEY: Ah fuhnik Stuhvuh. (I'm fucking starving.)

TWYLA: You're finding yourself really amusing aren't you?

JOEY: Yuh! Ah um.

JOEY LAUGHS UPROARIOUSLY, VERY HIGH. LIGHTS RISE ON JAKE AND ROBYN AT THE SEX APARTMENT. THEY'RE IN THE PULL-OUT BED.

JAKE: I'm so sorry.

ROBYN: Have you finally gotten bored with me?

JAKE: No. I – I can't sleep. My back and legs get this really strange ache.

ROBYN: So it was the pain?

JAKE: I just sort of – lost sensation. Who knows what I've done to my back moving Joey around all these years?

THEY GET OUT OF BED, DRESS, STRAIGHTEN THE ROOM ETC.

ROBYN: Children aren't meant to be a lifelong commitment.

JAKE: Yes they are.

ROBYN: Not full-time. If you don't take some time for yourself you'll burn out.

JAKE: What do you think tonight is?

ROBYN: But still you need someone to help you deal with the physical challenges. Someone –

JAKE: Younger? Stronger.

ROBYN: Yes.

PAUSE .

JAKE: Are you writing?

ROBYN: No. You?

JAKE: I'm still having trouble concentrating.

ROBYN: *River Run Rapid* was an amazing novel.

JAKE: Nearly twenty years ago.

ROBYN: It's not too late to write another.

JAKE: That was the plan.

ROBYN: Until Joey?

JAKE: Until Viola and mom got hit by that drunk. With everyone helping I might've found the time to peck something out but after that –

ROBYN: What do you want Jake?

JAKE: Want?

ROBYN: Now. For yourself.

JAKE: I have a severely disabled son. I have no self.

ROBYN: Have you ever read Joey your novel?

JAKE: No.

ROBYN: Why not?

JAKE: He's never been much on anything involving reading. And the book –

ROBYN: Is about a creative young man whose first child is about to be born.

JAKE: How would I explain the ending to him? All children are perfect. That's the final line.

ROBYN: I didn't mean to take this anywhere morbid.

JAKE: I'm just another guy who turned out one good novel before his life took some unexpected turns. A few of them good. Like you.

ROBYN: Your class took me from gifted amateur to marginally skilled amateur.

JAKE: You could go much farther.

ROBYN: I like exactly where I am. I have my hard working withholding husband two civic committees two hot yoga classes the readers group a couple of sons and you. It's quite enough.

JAKE: So you're settling?

ROBYN: I settled years ago. These meetings have come to mean so much to me. Your friendship.

JAKE: Friendship?

ROBYN: You know if our situations were different –

JAKE: But they're not.

ROBYN: No. That was always part of the deal.

JAKE: So we've always said.

ROBYN: You're not implying –

JAKE: And if I were?

ROBYN: But you're not.

PAUSE.

JAKE: I'll get something to help with my erection.

ROBYN: Please.

JAKE EXITS. LIGHTS RISE ON TWYLA WHO IS TIDYING UP THE LIVING ROOM. JAKE ENTERS.

TWYLA: Who won?

JAKE: No one. How was Joey?

TWYLA: Smoking dope with Rowdy.

JAKE: They do that.

TWYLA: You don't mind?

JAKE: It doesn't seem to have any negative effects on him.

TWYLA: His doctor –

JAKE: Doesn't think it's an issue. How are you doing?

TWYLA: Fine.

JAKE: Work's not too stressful?

TWYLA: Of course. We're just meat cogs in a corporate machine.

JAKE: What about the Hispanic guy?

TWYLA: Hector. Jesus Jake. He's disappeared. After nearly a year. He didn't even text me or break-up in an email like they usually do

JAKE: You might be happier as a lesbian.

TWYLA: I barely have time to be a straight person.

JAKE: What've you had to drink?

TWYLA: Coupla glasses of wine. Don't sweat it.

JAKE: You sure?

TWYLA: Yeah. Are you okay?

JAKE: I'm just – I'm really tired. Can you lock up when you go?

TWYLA: Sure.

JAKE: Thanks.

JAKE EXITS. TWYLA PUNCHES A NUMBER OF DIGITS INTO HER COMMUNICATIONS DEVICE AND WAITS FOR AN ANSWER. HECTOR'S RECORDED MESSAGE IS HEARD DISTANTLY.

TWYLA: Fuck you Hector. Fuck you and die.

TWYLA TURNS THE LIGHTS OUT AND EXITS. LIGHTS RISE ON JAKE, SLEEPING. HE SITS UP SUDDENLY, PANICKED.

JAKE: Joey. Son don't. Oh shit. What the – shit –

ROBYN APPEARS IN THE DOORWAY OF THE SEX APARTMENT WITH A TRAY OF TEA. JAKE IS IN THE PULL-OUT BED.

ROBYN: Are you alright?

JAKE: What time is it?

ROBYN: Quite early.

JAKE GETS OUT OF BED. HE'S HALF DRESSED. HE STRAIGHTENS HIMSELF UP.

JAKE: Was it okay?

ROBYN: It verged on great.

JAKE: Good thing I'm seeing my doc so much these days.

ROBYN: What's happening?

JAKE: Do you have an idea how old it makes you feel to go for an MRI in a nearly empty hospital at three a.m.? They do that now because there are so many of us – continuous twenty-four hour medical testing.

ROBYN: That must be terrible for your sleep cycle.

JAKE: I just dreamed about Joey but he wasn't disabled. He was tall and perfect and very smart. He was saying something about me having a tail.

ROBYN: You've both got big things on your minds.

JAKE: Like his boner.

ROBYN: Exactly.

JAKE: He doesn't want any of the options The Services offers.

ROBYN: They do that?

JAKE: Yeah.

ROBYN: At his age?

JAKE: Sexual feelings don't start at 18. He feels so ugly and he is so misshapen – but I – I just hate thinking about the things he'll never experience.

ROBYN: Are you considering – ?

JAKE: No.

ROBYN: I know most people wouldn't understand –

JAKE: Don't.

ROBYN: Horrible to consider.

JAKE: Beyond.

ROBYN: But still –

JAKE: Please.

ROBYN: You wipe him after shitting – hold his dick for him when he pisses – clean his foreskin – is a quick hand job really that different?

JAKE: If it were one of your sons would you do it?

ROBYN: Not if he was straight. That's too dangerous. I'd get his father to do it. But if he was gay I'd do it.

JAKE: I'm not – does that make sense?

ROBYN: If the child's too attracted it can take on unnecessarily erotic overtones. But when the parent and child have the same orientation it really isn't that much more intimate than the many intimate things you do with him already.

JAKE: I just – I can't –

ROBYN: Because it's sexual?

JAKE: Yes!

ROBYN: Pent up sexual desire does horrible things to men.

JAKE: But I – I – I – I can't – can't jack – masturbate my son. I can't. It steps over too many lines. And if anyone found out – they could arrest me for child abuse incest – whatever. They could take Joey away.

ROBYN: These are exceptional circumstances Jake.

JAKE: I'm never quite sure what Joey's incapable of doing and what he just doesn't want to do himself.

ROBYN   That comes from being a teenager.

JAKE: Am I a terrible parent because I can't masturbate my disabled son?

ROBYN: No. And we have to go.

JAKE: Good night.

ROBYN: You were great.

          THEY KISS. JAKE EXITS AS THE LIGHTS RISE ON A PARK. ROWDY IS WALKING WITH JOEY.

ROWDY: Look at the way the light's hittin' the water in the fountain. It's like shafts of diamonds or shit.

JOEY: Hush muh ush. (Hurts my eyes.)

ROWDY: Where's your cap bro?

JOEY: Muh casp ih muh pug. (My cap's in my pack.)

ROWDY: Gotcha.

JOEY: Huhup. Ih huhs. (Hurry up. It hurts.)

ROWDY: Calm down Jerusalem.

JOEY: Cuh uh! Huhup. (Come on! Hurry up.)

          ROWDY GETS THE CAP FROM THE PACK AND PUTS IT ON JOEY AS HE SPEAKS.

ROWDY: There ya go.

JOEY: Sankoo.

ROWDY: You an' me could do this every day bud.

JOEY: Wah?

ROWDY: Hang out. A nice long walk – maybe a movie or a Megadeth concert or something.

JOEY: Mayahduh ih plang?! (Megadeth is playing?!)

ROWDY: I mean if they like came to town. If you had your own place. With me.

JOEY: Uh yuh.

ROWDY: You talked to your dad right?

PAUSE.

ROWDY: Joe!

JOEY: Eeh muh dah. Ee dun wun muh tah guh. (He's my dad. He doesn't want me to go.)

ROWDY: That's what he says but he's not getting any tail til you're out of the house bud.

JOEY: Weewee? (Really?)

ROWDY: Ladies don't fuck men with kids let alone fucked up kids.

JOEY: Ee dunoh sum weewah wuwud abud susk. (He doesn't seem very worried about sex.)

ROWDY: All guys want sex.

JOEY'S TABLET BUZZES. HE STABS A BUTTON.

JOEY: Dah!

JAKE IS HEARD FROM THE TABLET.

JAKE: Where are you?

JOEY: Dugwuh pah. (Dogwood Park.)

JAKE: You didn't get off the school bus.

JOEY: Ih wuh nie. Wuh wunnah tah wah. (It was nice. We wanted to walk.)

ROWDY: We're just around the corner Mr Sturdy.

JAKE: You're supposed to call –

JOEY: Ah fuguh. (I forgot.)

ROWDY: I can see you from here.

JAKE: Where?

ROWDY WAVES.

ROWDY: Right here.

JOEY: Buh dah.

JOEY DISCONNECTS FROM THE PHONE JUST AS JAKE ENTERS, PUTTING AWAY HIS COMMUNICATIONS DEVICE.

JAKE: What were you thinking?

ROWDY: It's so sunny and Joe wanted to walk.

JAKE: If you'd called –

JOEY: Ah fuhguh! (I forgot.)

ROWDY: I gotta fat snatch I gotta report to. I'll call you tomorrow Joe.

JOEY: Oh tesk muh. (Or text me.)

ROWDY: Remember.

JOEY: Yuh.

ROWDY: Good-bye Mr Sturdy.

JAKE: Bye now.

ROWDY SHAKES JAKE'S HAND FIRMLY, HUGS JOEY AND EXITS.

JAKE: How was school?

JOEY: Ah had ih. Ah ahwuz had ih. (I hate it. I always hate it.)

JAKE: It's never been your thing.

JOEY: Zih juz peepuh don shuh wiv dah hunsh. (It's just people doing shit with their hands.)

JAKE: And their brains. You have to use your brain.

JOEY: *(BRANDISHES HIS TABLET AT JAKE.)* Mujuh wums hups muh bwen. (Magic Worms helps my brain.)

JAKE: It's just a few more months.

JOEY: Ah dah wah? (And then what?)

JAKE: You'll still have physical therapy three times a week and there are some special courses I've been looking into –

JOEY: Wuh kanah cusush? (What kinda courses?)

JAKE: There's a computer course designed for people with special physical needs –

JOEY: Muh skuh? (More school?)

JAKE: Well what would you like to do when you're finished school?

JOEY: Ah wunuh muh owd. (I want to move out.)

JAKE: What?

JOEY: Wowdee un ah. Wuh cuh geh ah pash tahgeda. (Rowdy and I. We could get a place together.)

JAKE: Rowdy could never take care of you.

JOEY: Yuh wuh duh hup uf duh Suhvashush. (Yes with the help of the Services.)

JAKE: But you have our house and your own room and everything set up to help you.

JOEY: Tuh Suhvash hah ah plah luh thuh. (The Services has a place like that.)

JAKE: Buddy The Services isn't the magical helper you and Rowdy think it is. Without my salary our lives would be much harder. We can barely meet our needs right now. And who's going to shop and pay the bills and run out for medications – ?

JOEY: Wowdee.

JAKE: Joey why do you want to leave home?

JOEY: Wowdee shesh wuh kun fun ah ply – (Rowdy says
         we can find a place –)

JAKE: I don't care what Rowdy says. I need to know why
         you want to leave me.

         PAUSE.

JAKE: Joey?

JOEY: Uh wuh tuh buh lah nohmuh pupuh. (I want to be
         like normal people.)

JAKE: I understand that. But –

JOEY: Uh duh wunuh lub wiv yuh fuhufuh dah. (I don't
         wanna live with you forever dad.)

         LONG PAUSE.

JAKE: Let's talk about it again when you graduate.

JOEY: Nuh.

JAKE: Joey.

JOEY: Ah wun yuh tah teh muh ah cuh mub owd nuh. (I
         want you to tell me I can move out now.)

JAKE: We'll talk about it later.

JOEY: Nuh!

JAKE: What's the deal?

JOEY: Yuh azah tuh muh wuh dah dew! (You always tell
         me what to do.)

JAKE: I'm your dad. That's my job.

JOEY: Onuh fuh unudah yuh. (Only for another year.)

JAKE: Let's just head home.

JOEY: Fuh yuh! (Fuck you!)

JAKE: Don't talk to me like that.

JOEY: Ah gon muh owd uh muh und und ooh cah sop muh! (I'm gonna move out on my own and you can't stop me!)

JAKE: You're acting like a child.

JOEY: Nuh ah nud. (No I'm not.)

JAKE GRABS JOEY'S CHAIR. JOEY TRIES TO MOVE AWAY.

JAKE: You're not going anywhere.

JOEY: Yuh uh fuhuh ashuh! (You're a fucking asshole!)

JAKE: Joey stop –

JOEY LASHES OUT HARD WITH HIS ARM, STRIKING JAKE ACROSS THE CHEST. JAKE FALLS TO THE GROUND, ONTO HIS BACK, VERY HARD. HE SCREAMS IN AGONY.

JOEY: Dah!

JAKE: Jesus fucking son of a bitch!

JOEY: Dah.

JAKE: Shitty slutbag whore!

JOEY: Wuh ih uh?

JAKE: Oh my fucking god! Oh fuck!

JOEY HITS THE EMERGENCY NUMBER ON HIS PAD. A WOMAN'S VOICE IS HEARD FROM THE PAD.

VOICE: Emergency services. Your present location and number have been entered into the system. What is the nature of your emergency please?

JOEY: Sumush wan wiv muh dah! (Something's wrong with my dad.)

VOICE: I beg your pardon?

JAKE SCREAMS.

JOEY: Seh uh albumas. (Send an ambulance.)

VOICE: Sir are you drunk?

JOEY: Nuh! Muh dah ih hud. (No! My dad is hurt.)

VOICE: I can't understand what you're saying.

JOEY: Ah cuh tah ruh. (I can't talk right.)

VOICE: Please repeat.

JOEY: *(WITH GREAT EFFORT.)* Am-bu-last!

VOICE: You need an ambulance?

JOEY: Yuh!

VOICE: An ambulance has been dispatched. Please stay
           on the line. Does anyone need CPR or emergency
           care?

JOEY: Yuh! Ebuhwuh! (Yes! Everyone!)

           *JAKE MOANS IN AGONY. BLACKOUT. A LIGHT RISES ON
           ROBYN IN THE SEX APARTMENT. SHE CHECKS THE
           TIME AND MOVES TO THE WINDOW, LOOKING OUT, HER
           COMMUNICATION DEVICE SOUNDS.*

ROBYN: Jake? Where are you?

JAKE: The hospital.

ROBYN: What?

JAKE: Saint Something.

ROBYN: Are you okay?

           *A LIGHT RISES ON JAKE IN HIS HOSPITAL ROOM. HE'S
           DRESSED TO GO HOME.*

JAKE: It's called spinal stenosis.

ROBYN: I've never heard of that.

JAKE: It's fairly common in the elderly but seems to be
           hitting me sooner than usual. Basically there are
           bone spurs growing into my spinal column and
           cutting off the nerves to other parts of my body.

ROBYN: What causes it?

JAKE: They don't really know. It's distributed pretty evenly
           throughout my spine – it's doing something to my
           arms and legs and it affects my brain stem as well.

ROBYN: I'll Google it. Are you going to be okay?

JAKE: Of course.

ROBYN: Jake –

TWYLA AND JOEY ENTER.

JAKE: I've got to go. I'll call you when I can.

ROBYN: Please.

JAKE: Sorry.

JAKE HANGS UP. THE LIGHT ON ROBYN GOES OUT.

TWYLA: Is there a lot of pain?

JAKE: Yes. A lot.

TWYLA: Painkillers?

JAKE: Mega.

TWYLA: They can fix it right?

JAKE: Joey why don't you go out to the nurse's station and ask her for the bag with my valuables in it?

JOEY: Dah buh? (The bag?)

JAKE: At the end of the hall.

JOEY: Ruh. (Right.)

JAKE: Thank you.

JOEY EXITS.

JAKE: He isn't going to take long so please just listen to me. No one seems to know exactly what this thing is going to do to me and how fast it's going to do it. It could be serious.

TWYLA: There must be other options – Holistic treatments. Homeopathy. Acupuncture.

JAKE: Witch doctors? Yoga instructors. No. The science is pretty clear on this one.

TWYLA: Times like this I wish we believed in god.

JAKE: Wouldn't change a thing.

TWYLA: Could it be fatal?

JAKE: No. Just debilitating.

TWYLA: Thankfully.

JAKE: Yes. The thought of Joey being on his own –

TWYLA: Jake I wouldn't let that happen.

          PAUSE.

JAKE: We were fighting. He pushed me.

TWYLA: Why were you fighting?

JAKE: He wants to move into an assisted living apartment
          with Rowdy.

TWYLA: What?

JAKE: I won't be able to care for him the same way.

TWYLA: So what – Joey moves in with a pervert and you –
          lie in bed and cry?

JAKE: If I can't take care of myself The Services will send
          someone who can.

TWYLA: Jake the government has hacked The Services to the
          bone. There's no other help –

JAKE: Twyla –

          *JOEY ENTERS WITH A GYM BAG CONTAINING JAKE'S
          THINGS.*

JOEY: Gud hum. (Got them.)

JAKE: Thanx son. We can go home now.

JOEY: Yuh suh yuh hokah? (You're sure you're okay?)

JAKE: Yes.

TWYLA: I'll take the suitcase. Can you walk?

JAKE: Short distances aren't such a problem.

JOEY: Hun unuh muh chuh. (Hang onto my chair.)

JAKE: *(HANGING ONTO THE CHAIR.)* Excellent idea.

JOEY: Un Tuhluh tuh hus otruh ahm. (Aunt Twyla take his other arm.)

TWYLA ASSISTS JAKE.

TWYLA: Got him.

JOEY: Lush guh hum. (Let's go home.)

A LIGHT RISES ON ROBYN ON HER COMMUNICATION DEVICE IN THE SEX APARTMENT.

ROBYN: Hey sorry. I know you're sick – not sick – disabled – wounded – whatever. I'm actually calling from Anastasia's. I keep coming here Tuesdays. I don't know why. Probably should've actually learned to play bridge. Ha ha. I dreamed about you. We were married and had cherubic red devil children in diapers with little pitchforks. It was quite wonderful. I miss you Jake. I hope you're well. Call me. Whenever you can.

LIGHTS RISE ON JAKE AND JOEY IN THE BATHROOM. JOEY'S IN THE TUB.

JOEY: Dah?

JAKE: Yeah?

JOEY: Ah suruh. (I'm sorry.)

JAKE: Joey –

JOEY: Fuh pusuh yuh duh. (For pushing you down.)

JAKE: That was a very bad thing to do. You know that. But the doctor's said something would've triggered the pain eventually.

JOEY: Ah dunuh buhk yuh bahg? (I didn't break your back?)

JAKE: They say this has been growing in me for a long time.

JOEY: Suh yuh buns uh fuht ub tuh? (So your bones are fucked up too?)

JAKE: I guess so.

JOEY: Wuh? (Why?)

JAKE: Who knows?

JOEY: Luf sugs. (Life sucks.)

JAKE: So I was thinking –

JOEY: Wuh?

JAKE: You should get that place with Rowdy.

JOEY: Ah nuh wuhnuh moob owd nuh muh. (I don't want to move out no more.)

JAKE: Why not?

JOEY: Huss gwunuh tah cah uf yuh? (Who's gonna take care of you?)

JAKE: Aunt Twyla. My friends –

JOEY: Wuh fwunsh? (What friends?)

JAKE: The Services will help out. I called Phillip. He's happy to work with both of us.

JOEY: Ah dun fing ah shuh moob owd nuh. (I don't think I should move out now.)

JAKE: No seriously –

JOEY: Nuh. Ah stuh wiv yuh. (No. I'll stay with you.)

JAKE: Joey –

JOEY: Ih muh fawh! (It's my fault!)

JAKE: Don't cry.

JOEY: Uh suruh dah. (I'm sorry dad.)

JAKE: It's okay.

JAKE SOOTHES JOEY.

JOEY: Uh guh mah un uh cand kohtroh ih. (I get mad and I can't control it.)

JAKE: It's not your fault.

JOEY: Uh suh suhuh. Wuh duh ah gud suh cayshuh? (I'm so sorry. Why do I get so crazy?)

JAKE: It's your age. It's very confusing. We'll figure this out. It's okay.

PAUSE. JOEY GETS HIMSELF UNDER CONTROL AS JAKE WASHES HIM.

JOEY: Wiw yuh buh alba tuh wuhk? (Will you be able to work?)

JAKE: Sure.

JOEY: Weh tash guh. (Well that's good.)

JAKE: It is.

JOEY: Muhbuh Wowdee kud heb ush. (Maybe Rowdy could help us.)

JAKE: Let me think about it.

JOEY: Ah kah hub tuh. (I can help too.)

JAKE: Don't worry son.

PAUSE. JOEY IS BREATHING VERY HEAVILY. HIS EYES ARE CLOSED. JAKE RINSES THE LAST OF THE SOAP FROM HIS BODY.

JOEY: Bonuh.

JAKE: Yes.

JOEY: Suruh

JAKE: Completely normal.

JOEY: Nuh wuhmuh wuh ufuh tuh muh. Weh uh fik ubuh ud ih ih mag muh kashuh. (No woman will ever touch me. When I think about it it makes me crazy.)

PAUSE.

JAKE: I'll take care of you Joey. No matter what. Always.

JOEY: Uh duh wuhuh buh hew wihow ooh dah. (I don't want to be here without you dad.)

JAKE: Do you mean that?

JOEY: Suh.

JAKE: If I had to – go away – you'd want to come with me?

JOEY: Yuh.

PAUSE.

JAKE: Joe I – I can help – help you if you need it.

JOEY: Heb muh? (Help me?)

JAKE: If you – you need me to. It's like washing your hair or changing your underwear. If you want me to. You don't have to say anything. Just turn away if you don't want me to. Do you understand?

JOEY CAN'T LOOKS HIS FATHER IN THE EYE.

JAKE: I want you to close your eyes.

JOEY: Uhkuh.

JAKE: Now put your hand on mine.

JOEY: Dah?

JAKE: You've been looking at some – some naked ladies on your tablet right?

JOEY: Yuh.

JAKE: Is there one you really like?

JOEY: Yuh. Duh blun huh duh unuh. (Yes. The blond who does anal.)

JAKE: Think of her.

JOEY: Suh.

JAKE: This is not me. It's you. I'm not here.

JOEY: Uhkuh

THESE ACTIONS ARE NOT SEEN BECAUSE THEY HAPPEN BELOW THE EDGE OF THE TUB BUT THEY ARE CLEAR.

JAKE: This is you.

JAKE TAKES HOLD OF JOEY'S COCK. JOEY GASPS.

JAKE: Or that girl.

JOEY SMILES AND MAKES A GURGLING SOUND AS JAKE MASTURBATES HIM.

JAKE: Just think of her.

JOEY: Yuh.

JAKE COVERS HIS FACE WITH HIS OTHER HAND.

JAKE: Think of her.

JOEY'S EYES CLOSE. JAKE FIGHTS NOT TO CRY. FADE TO BLACK. A MOMENT OF SILENCE. LIGHTS RISE ON THE KITCHEN. TWYLA ENTERS WITH ROWDY AND BAGS OF GROCERIES WHICH THEY UNPACK AS THE SCENE PROGRESSES.

ROWDY: I still say Fifth Street would've been faster.

TWYLA: There's construction on Fifth.

ROWDY: They finished it last week.

TWYLA: You didn't mention that.

ROWDY: I told you to take Fifth.

TWYLA: You didn't say the construction was finished.

ROWDY: Do I have to explain everything all the way through all the time?

TWYLA: Yes.

ROWDY: Because you think I'm stupid.

TWLYA: I don't think you're stupid.

ROWDY: You don't trust me.

TWYLA: I'm just not sure you being here is a great idea.

ROWDY: Mr S has the money Joey has the brains and I have the power. Works fine except I do most of everything.

JOEY ENTERS.

JOEY: Dih yuh guh muh tust? (Did you get my text?)

TWYLA: Halfway home. Sorry. You're not completely out are you?

JOEY: Nuh kut. (Not quite.)

ROWDY: What'd we forget?

TWYLA: Toilet paper. I'll get a crateful on my way here tomorrow.

JOEY: Uh muhd tuh puh Ih oh thuh Lish. Suruh. (I meant to put it on the list. Sorry.)

TWYLA: Where's Philip?

JOEY: Luf Ah shiks. (Left at six.)

TWYLA: Is it after six?

JOEY: Tunuh ufuh. Yuh guh duh bwah suruhlah? (Twenty after. You got the bran cereal?)

TWYLA: Extra bran.

JAKE ENTERS IN SWEATS AND A ROBE. HE USES A CANE. HIS ENERGY IS CLEARLY DIMISHED.

JAKE: It's a good day.

ROWDY: Why?

JAKE: I actually wiped my ass properly.

JAKE POURS HIMSELF A DRINK.

TWYLA: It's a bit early to be drinking.

JAKE: You're one to talk. Anyway I only sleep in drug-induced snatches so linear time really has no meaning to me.

TWYLA: You okay?

JAKE: Sure.

ROWDY PICKS UP A NUMBER OF ITEMS.

ROWDY: Stowin' shit.

ROWDY EXITS.

TWYLA: Teaching today?

JAKE: No. No I'm not. I – I won't be teaching anymore.

TWYLA: What?

JAKE: Apparently my last batch of assessments was incomprehensible. Although they made perfect sense to me at the time. The college has been very understanding of my – challenges but really had no choice blah blah blah.

TWYLA: I guess it's a good thing your medical insurance kicked in.

JAKE: I'll still have to apply for disability.

TWYLA: More forms. The two bowls on the counter are dinner. Just throw them in the microwave then split the container of mixed vegetables and you're set.

JAKE: Thank you.

TWYLA: Are you managing your pain alright?

JAKE: Yes but it makes me so dopey.

JOEY: Eeh kye ih hush seep. Uh heeh huh. (He cries in his sleep. I hear him.)

TWYLA: Did he eat a lunch?

JOEY: Eeh pish ah ih buh dun eeh mush. (He picks at it but doesn't eat much.)

TWYLA: He has to eat some real food.

JAKE: I'm fine.

TWYLA: Maybe I should move in for a while.

JOEY: Nuh!

JAKE: We've got Rowdy.

TWYLA: Okay but really –

           ROWDY ENTERS

ROWDY: Who needs tea?

TWYLA: No one.

           THERE'S A KNOCK AT THE DOOR.

JOEY: Wuh?

ROWDY: Got it.

           ROWDY HOLLERS AT THE DOOR.

ROWDY: Come in.

           ROBYN ENTERS.

ROBYN: Hello.

JAKE: Robyn?

TWYLA: Robyn?

ROBYN: Hi. Yes. I'm Robyn. With a Y.

TWYLA: Wouldn't that be Yobin?

ROBYN: Instead of the i.

TWYLA: Right.

ROBYN: I'm one of Jake's former students. I heard he'd
           had some trouble so I thought since I was in the
           neighbourhood anyway that I'd stop by and say
           hello.

JAKE: Hello.

ROBYN: Hello.

           PAUSE.

JAKE: This is my sister Twyla – my son Joey and –

ROWDY: *(MOVING TO ROBYN TO SHAKE HER HAND.)* Rowdy
           Akers. No real relation. Charmed to meet you mam.

ROBYN: I've come at a bad time haven't I?

JAKE: It's fine. Joey and Rowdy – I know you guys have things to do.

ROWDY: Let's give your old dad some privacy.

JOEY: Uh. Yuh. *(TO ROBYN.)* Nih tuh mute ooh Wubuh. (Nice to meet you Robyn.)

ROBYN: Pardon?

JAKE: He said it's nice to meet you Robyn.

ROBYN: Of course. Sorry. It's nice to meet you too Joey.

          JOEY AND ROWDY EXIT.

TWYLA: You and Jake have stayed in touch all these years?

ROBYN: Sporadically. I have my own family to look after. Thank god for the internet.

TWYLA: The only people I've ever known Jake to hang with are some of the buddies he plays hockey with.

ROBYN: Good for him for staying active.

TWYLA: Yeah it's funny.

ROBYN: What?

TWYLA: Hockey every Tuesday night for years and he never seemed to – get into better shape.

ROBYN: At least his heart is healthy.

TWYLA: Yes.

JAKE: I'll play hockey again.

ROBYN: Sure you will.

TWYLA: I should – run. Nice to meet you Robyn.

ROBYN: Lovely to meet you.

TWYLA: Have a great game.

          TWYLA EXITS.

ROBYN: Are we that obvious?

JAKE: Apparently.

ROBYN: I had to know how you're doing.

JAKE: It's okay.

ROBYN: Have you missed me?

JAKE: Yes of course but –

ROBYN: What?

JAKE: This thing occupies a huge space in my life now.

ROBYN: Don't the painkillers help?

JAKE: They don't kill pain so much as they kill my ability to care about pain – and anything else.

ROBYN: Do you mind if I have a drink?

JAKE: No. Fresh mine up too while you're at it.

ROBYN: Is that such a good idea?

JAKE: It is an excellent idea.

ROBYN: Would you like to do something? A game – cards? Some light oral perhaps?

    PAUSE.

ROBYN: Or heavier oral if you prefer.

JAKE: Unfortunately the nerve attacks go through my dick. Sometimes I get these completely unexpected and inappropriate hard-ons without even knowing it's happening and other times it's like I'm dead below the waist. Even if I got hard I wouldn't be able to come. That's the meds.

ROBYN: I'm sorry.

JAKE: It's made masturbating Joey easier.

ROBYN: So you've –

JAKE: He goes into whatever fantasy he's discovered on the net and I make myself dead inside.

ROBYN: Oh Jake –

JAKE: All in a day's work.

ROBYN I did some research Jake. I know how serious stenosis can be.

JAKE: But it can also be just annoying for some.

ROBYN: You seem – more than annoyed.

JAKE: Yes.

ROBYN MOVES BEHIND JAKE AND MASSAGES HIS SHOULDERS.

ROBYN: I wish there was some way I could help.

JAKE: That feels so good.

ROBYN: Just relax.

JAKE: I never wanted you to see this dump.

ROBYN: It's a well-used family home.

JAKE: It's filthy. There are tire marks on every wall. The furniture's falling apart. The windows haven't been cleaned in –

ROBYN: Jake all I see is you.

PAUSE.

JAKE: How are the boys?

ROBYN: Men now and completely uninterested in me. Anastasia's taken to coming home early because she knows I'm there alone. She's very sympathetic and it's nice to have someone to talk to but she's not you. I miss you – your voice your skin the way we – are you sleeping?

HE HAS FALLEN ASLEEP. SHE KISSES THE TOP OF HIS HEAD.

ROBYN: I'll see myself out.

           JOEY ENTERS.

JOEY: Ah yuh lufuh? (Are you leaving?)

ROBYN: No. I'm leaving.

           JOEY NODS.

ROBYN: Your dad fell asleep.

JOEY: Guh. Eeh uh ahpyah wuh huh seeb. Uh wuk hum
           ub fuh dunuh. (Good. He is happier when he sleeps.
           I'll wake him up for dinner.)

ROBYN: *(NO IDEA WHAT HE'S SAID.)* Yes right.

JOEY: Yuh uh vewuh nesh tuh luh uh. (You are very nice
           to look at.)

ROBYN: Good.

JOEY: Ooh hub nuh uduh whuh um suhuh. (You have no
           idea what I'm saying.)

ROBYN: Say good-bye for me.

JOEY: *(WITH GREAT EFFORT TO BE UNDERSTOOD.)* Preash
           cub bag.

ROBYN: Did you just say please come back?

JOEY: Yuh.

ROBYN: You think that's a good idea?

JOEY: *(WITH EFFORT.)* Eeh hush nuh frunsh. (He has no
           friends.)

ROBYN: Sorry?

JOEY: Eeh neesh frunsh. Pleesh. (He needs friends. Please.)

           PAUSE.

ROBYN: It was nice to meet you.

JOEY: Ooh tuh. (You too.)

ROBYN EXITS. LIGHTS ON THE KITCHEN RISE. TWYLA IS AT THE FRIDGE, CLEANING IT OUT. SHE TSKS IN DISGUST. ROWDY ENTERS WITH A BAG.

ROWDY: I got the meds. And rye.

TWYLA: Nearly everything in this fridge is moldy.

ROWDY: There's a lot of hair in it too. Creeps me out.

TWYLA: You can't let it get like this.

ROWDY: It's self-cleaning. So's the stove.

TWYLA: That doesn't mean –

ROWDY: Says it right on the cover of both manuals. I looked. Self-cleaning.

TWYLA: When you moved in you said you'd help out.

ROWDY: Why can't that be your job?

TWYLA: Because I'm already doing the laundry. Jesus this is disgusting.

ROWDY: Need another bag?

TWYLA: I might.

ROWDY GETS HER ANOTHER GARBAGE BAG.

ROWDY: I'll tell Joe. Where's Mr Sturdy?

TWYLA: Having a lie down.

ROWDY: Joey?

TWYLA: Playing with his pad somewhere.

ROWDY: I'm just gonna leave the pills here so you can divide them into their pill things.

TWYLA: Sure.

SHE TAKES THE BUCKET TO THE SINK AND EMPTIES IT.

ROWDY: Want me to crack the CC?

TWYLA: I wouldn't say no.

ROWDY: Really?

TWYLA: We're all adults.

ROWDY BRINGS HER A GLASS OF WATER, OPENS THE BOTTLE AND POURS SOME RYE INTO A TUMBLER.

TWYLA: Is this better for you? Living here?

ROWDY: The group home was a nightmare. There was this guy there that screamed all night long. Every night. They gave him pills but they only worked for a few hours eh. I swear some nights I wanted to stab that fucking kid in the throat just to stop him from making those sounds.

JOEY ENTERS.

JOEY: Wowdee whuh huh yuh buhn? (Rowdy where have you been?)

ROWDY: Getting the stuff you told me to get.

JOEY: Whuh duhn ooh cuh suh muh? (Why didn't you come see me?)

ROWDY: What's the emerg?

JOEY: Dah nuh hih mesh. (Dad needs his meds)

ROWDY: In twenty minutes. I know how to tell time bitch.

JOEY: Duh cuh muh buch. (Don't call me a bitch.)

ROWDY: Then don't act like one Loretta.

TWYLA: Joey someone has to check the fridge for old food.

JOEY HAS HIS TABLET READY.

JOEY: Huh Uhfuh? (How often?)

TWYLA: Every three days for sure.

JOEY: Ahl ud ih tuh Wowdeesh shorsh. (I'll add it to Rowdy's chores.)

JOEY TYPES INTO THE TABLET WITH AMAZING DEXTERITY GIVEN HIS MALFORMED HANDS.

ROWDY: I'm not a slave you know.

JOEY: Ho shuh hub. (Oh shut up.)

TWYLA: I need another drink.

JOEY: Duh guh pushed uv yuh druvuh. (Don't get pissed if you're driving.)

TWYLA: I'm hardly pissed.

ROWDY: She's earned a couple drinks.

JAKE ENTERS. HE LOOKS VERY TIRED.

JAKE: I could really use a glass of water.

ROWDY: Got it.

JAKE: What time is it?

JOEY: Fuh. (Four.)

TWYLA: Why don't we go sit on the deck? You could really use some sun.

JAKE: Naw.

JAKE SITS AT THE TABLE.

TWYLA: Let me comb your hair.

JAKE: I'm fine.

TWYLA: Happy to do it.

JAKE: Lay off the fucking hair.

TWYLA: Okay.

JOEY: Ah yuh hunguh duh? (Are you hungry dad?)

JAKE: No. Just thirsty.

ROWDY GIVES JAKE WATER.

ROWDY: Here you go Mr S.

JAKE: It smells different in here.

TWYLA: I cleaned the fridge.

JAKE: How are you?

TWYLA: Okay.

JOEY: Uh yuh ruduh fuh yuh punkuhush? (Are you ready for your painkillers?)

JAKE: I'm okay for a few more minutes. How's it going Rowdy?

ROWDY: If you don't mind me saying so Mr Sturdy your family has been treating me like I'm some kind of slave or something and I'm gonna say I'm getting really sick of it.

JAKE: The Services does give you an extra allowance for helping out.

ROWDY: I know and I'm grateful. But there's a limit. I've got other things to do.

JOEY: Wuh uvuh thuns? (What other things.)

ROWDY: I need a social life. Romance.

TWYLA: You have almost every evening to yourself.

ROWDY: Yeah but I don't have no place I can bring a girl to or whatever.

JAKE: Rowdy if you had a steady girlfriend we could discuss it but I won't have you bringing random women into my home just for sex.

ROWDY: Why not?

TWYLA: They might steal something.

JOEY: Oh smoag cugaruh. (Or smoke cigarettes.)

ROWDY: I tolju I wouldn't pick up any smokers!

TWYLA: Go to their place.

ROWDY: They don't always have places. Some of them barely have things.

JAKE: Then get a motel room. Jesus fucking Christ this is our home not a halfway house for horny young men! Why can't you seem to get that?

ROWDY: Because I never had a home.

PAUSE.

JAKE: We appreciate everything you do here. I'm sorry if that isn't always clear.

ROWDY: No it's I didn't mean shit okay I'm sorry.

TWYLA: I ran into Sandro last week.

JAKE: How is he?

TWYLA: Fat and kind of sad. He asked how you were doing.

JAKE: What did you tell him?

TWYLA: The truth.

JAKE: Twyla –

TWYLA: When people ask I tell them you're having a health issue – that we have no idea how long it will last and that you're dealing with it as best you can. Isn't that right?

JAKE: Yes.

TWYLA: He gave me his card. I thought –

JAKE: Socializing isn't high on my agenda right now.

JOEY: Ih tum dah. (It's time dad.)

JAKE: Is it?

JOEY: Yuh.

ROWDY GETS JAKE HIS PILL AND SOME WATER AS HE SPEAKS.

ROWDY: Here you go.

JAKE: Great.

JAKE TAKES HIS PILL AND CHASES IT WITH SOME WATER.

JOEY: Ooh hunguh dah? (You hungry dad?)

JAKE: No.

TWYLA: I can warm you up some chow.

JAKE: I'm said I'm fine.

TWYLA: Just checking.

JOEY: Yul fee buduh wuh yuh pih kish ih. (You'll feel better when your pill kicks in.)

JAKE: Right.

JAKE EXITS.

ROWDY: You ready for something to eat?

JOEY: Nuh. Lesh guh tuh thuh puhc. (No. Let's go to the park.)

ROWDY: Naw.

JOEY: Yuh nufuh wunuh duh nufuh unuhmuh. (You never want to do nothing anymore.)

ROWDY: We'll go to the park tomorrow bud.

JOEY: Nuh shud. Ah huf ovuh frundsh. (No sweat. I have other friends.)

ROWDY: What other friends?

JOEY: *(BRANDISHES THE TABLET.)* Aw duh nud. (On the net.)

ROWDY: You think those are real friends?

JOEY: Uz weew uz ooh. Uhm nuhmuh un duh nuh. (As real as you. I'm normal on the net.)

JOEY EXITS ANGRILY. TWYLA UNLOADS JAKE AND JOEY'S WEEKLY PILL CONTAINERS, REMOVES A NUMBER OF PILL BOTTLES FROM THE BAG AND SEPARATES THEM INTO APPROPRIATE COMPARTMENTS.

ROWDY: Still working for that computer cult?

TWYLA: It's not a cult it's a corporation.

ROWDY: Everyone bows down to the mighty machine.

TWYLA: Gotta make a living.

ROWDY: You wanna drink?

TWYLA: I shouldn't.

ROWDY MIXES HER ANOTHER DRINK.

ROWDY: Got it.

TWYLA: Last one.

ROWDY: Sure. Hey Twyla can I talk to you about something just you know between us?

TWYLA: Is this something weird?

ROWDY: Pretty much yeah.

TWYLA: What?

ROWDY: So you know how Mr Sturdy jacks Joey off in the shower?

LONG PAUSE.

ROWDY: You didn't know that.

TWYLA: I – didn't.

ROWDY: It's not child molestering or anything weird like that. He's just helping him out you know the way any decent person would.

TWYLA: Right.

ROWDY: I guess that does sound kinda fucked up eh?

TWYLA: Yes but I – if I think about it – and I really don't want to – it's – you know – I – well I don't understand. No I do. No I don't.

ROWDY: No one else will do it and Joe can't do it himself because of his fucked up hands.

TWYLA: I'm – sad.

ROWDY: Sorry.

TWYLA: It's okay. I'm – what did you want to discuss?

ROWDY: Well Mr Sturdy's getting more and more frozen in his body and Joey's getting real moody because there's no more understanding hand jobs in the shower and I don't – I don't really see hand jobs as being part of my job description.

PAUSE.

TWYLA: Are you suggesting I should do it?

ROWDY: I mop up their piss.

TWYLA: *(HANDING HIM HER GLASS TO REFILL.)* Rowdy I can't even really even – think about this.

ROWDY: Yeah yeah. Got it. But I was thinking like maybe you know I might have recently met an open minded hooker who's not too expensive –

TWYLA: And this open-minded hooker would – ?

ROWDY: Give him something much wetter than a hand job from his dad.

TWYLA: We're really having this conversation right? I'm not – like having a stroke or something?

ROWDY: You need another drink.

TWYLA: I do.

ROWDY MAKES HER ANOTHER DRINK.

ROWDY: There's no one for me to talk about this shit with.

TWYLA: You think it would help? To bring this woman here?

ROWDY: Totally.

TWYLA: Then yes. Jesus. I can't – shit.

ROWDY: You want to smoke a joint.

HE LIGHTS A JOINT.

TWYLA: You're very intuitive.

ROWDY: Yes.

THEY SHARE THE JOINT.

ROWDY: Why don't you like people to touch you?

TWYLA: Who says – ?

ROWDY: I notice shit.

TWYLA: When people touch you or – you know – say they love you or make some kind of contact like that they always – they –

ROWDY: Want something?

TWYLA: The few times anyone's ever told me they love me it's right before or after they do something really horrible – or die. So yeah I'm not a big lover of love.

ROWDY: High?

TWYLA: Yeah you?

ROWDY: Totes.

TWYLA LAUGHS VERY HARD.

ROWDY: What?

TWYLA: That's so perfect. Totes. *(LAUGHS.)* Totes boats stoats –

ROWDY: It means totally.

TWYLA: I thought you meant like tote bags.

ROWDY: What the fuck are tote bags?

TWYLA: You know. Bags you – tote.

THEY BOTH LAUGH UPROARIOUSLY. IT PETERS OUT. THEY BREATHE HEAVILY. PAUSE.

TWYLA: I thought by now I'd have met a man who'd take me away from all this.

ROWDY: Where and when were you expecting that to happen?

TWYLA: At work like everyone else.

ROWDY KISSES HER SUDDENLY. SHE GIVES INTO IT THEN PULLS AWAY.

TWYLA: You really shouldn't –

ROWDY: When was the last time anyone made you feel good?

TWYLA: It's not really –

ROWDY: You deserve to feel good.

TWYLA: Rowdy.

THEY KISS AGAIN. JOEY ENTERS.

JOEY: Wuh duh fuh uh wunh wif ooh pupuh? (What the fuck is wrong with you people?)

ROWDY: Hey.

JOEY: Uh sith huh yuh tunk ooh shuh buh uktuh uh muh kuhchuh? (Is this how you think you should be acting in my kitchen?)

ROWDY: Thought you were busy.

JOEY: Yuh buh tutuh fuhuh ashulsh! (You're both total fucking assholes!)

TWYLA: Joey –

JOEY: Yuh uh owd laduh. (You're an old lady.)

TWYLA: I'm twenty-nine –

JOEY: Fuh yuh! (Fuck you!)

ROWDY: Don't talk to her like that.

TWYLA: Rowdy don't make it worse –

JAKE ENTERS GROGGY.

JAKE: Why are you shouting?

JOEY: Nuffuh. Fuhgud ud. (Nothing. Forget it.)

TWYLA: Just a –

ROWDY: Disagreement.

TWYLA: We didn't mean to wake you.

JAKE: I'm not sure if I was sleeping. I thought I was dreaming – I just – I heard this – uh –

JAKE'S EYES GROW WIDE. HE BEGINS TO MAKE A QUIET HUMMING SOUND, STARING STRAIGHT AHEAD. HE TWITCHES SLIGHTLY.

JOEY: Dah?

ROWDY: You okay?

JAKE JERKS SPASMODICALLY.

JOEY: Dah?!

ROWDY MOVES TO HELP JAKE.

ROWDY: Maybe you better –

JAKE FALLS TO THE GROUND, TWITCHING STIFFLY. THE NOISE HE'S MAKING HAS GOTTEN LOUDER. TWYLA FINDS HER COMMUNICATIONS DEVICE AND CALLS 911.

TWYLA: I need an ambulance immediately. Thank you.

ROWDY MOVES AND PUTS HIS HANDS UNDER JAKE'S HEAD SO HE DOESN'T BANG IT ON THE FLOOR.

ROWDY: I gotcha.

JOEY: Dah!

QUICK FADE TO BLACK. LIGHTS RISE ON ROBYN WALKING DOWN THE STREET WITH A SHOPPING BAG. HER COMMUNICATIONS DEVICE SOUNDS. SHE ANSWERS IT.

ROBYN: Hello? Who? Oh yes. Of course. Is there something wrong? His brain? Is he back in the – I see. Is it a coma? Conscious but immobile. Don't like the sound of that. Do you think there's any point in me – Right. Good. I appreciate you keeping me updated. That's very considerate Twyla. Call me if anything changes.

A LIGHT RISES ON A MEN'S BATHROOM. IN THE HOSPITAL JOEY IS STANDING AT A URINAL, HIS BACK TO THE AUDIENCE. ROWDY ASSISTS HIM BY UNDOING JOEY'S ZIPPER.

JOEY: Dah dun lug suh guh. (Dad don't look so good.)

ROWDY: I fucking hate fucking hospitals.

JOEY: Tay ih ud. (Take it out.)

ROWDY: I'm taking it out but you're gonna hold it the way I showed you.

JOEY: Ah truch. (I twitch.)

ROWDY: Try to keep your hands still.

JOEY: Ah cand. (I can't.)

ROWDY: Breathe steady.

JOEY CLUMSILY HOLDS HIS OWN DICK.

JOEY: Ah tuh. (I'll try.)

ROWDY: Concentrate.

JOEY: Ah uhm. (I am.)

PAUSE. NOTHING HAPPENS. ROWDY WHISTLES A COUPLE OF BARS OF SOMETHING TO MOVE THINGS ALONG. JOEY BEGINS TO PEE.

ROWDY: Yes!

JOEY: Eh. (Hey.)

ROWDY: Hold it steady. Aim for the cake thing. That's right.

JOEY: Uhm pung buh musuv. (I'm peeing by myself.)

ROWDY: Excellent.

JOEY: Nuh Shuh ih uv. (Now shake it off.)

ROWDY: What?

JOEY: Wew uh kuhd. (Well I can't.)

ROWDY: Oh for –

ROWDY QUICKLY SHAKES JOEY'S DICK OFF, RETURNS IT TO HIS PANTS AND ZIPS HIS FLY.

ROWDY: There. Happy?

JOEY: Chuh. (Chair.)

ROWDY: Right.

ROWDY ASSISTS JOEY BACK INTO THE CHAIR.

ROWDY: I think we might have to go back to the diaper thing.

JOEY: Nuh.

ROWDY: You still got some piss all over the front of your pants.

JOEY: Nuh deepah!

ROWDY: You don't leave me a lot of choice.

JOEY: Shuh huh. Fuh yuh. (Shut up. Fuck you.)

ROWDY: No fuck you. And while we're on the subject what I do with my dick is none of your business.

JOEY: Ah nuvuh suh id wush. (I never said it was.)

ROWDY: I'm talking about your whole scene when you walked in on me and Twyla.

JOEY: Yuh dun nuduh duh dath ihuh kishuh. (You don't need to do that in the kitchen.)

ROWDY: You're just fucking jealous.

JOEY: Fuh yuh. (Fuck you.)

ROWDY: I can get someone to help you Joe.

JOEY: Nuh!

ROWDY: You think you're the worst thing anyone's seen? There are kids in China born with skin like elephants and no legs. There are kids in Russia who shit through their mouths and piss out of their noses because of some nuclear thing. Are you worse off than those people?

JOEY: Shuh hub! (Shut up!)

JOEY SWINGS AT ROWDY. ROWDY KNOCKS HIS HAND AWAY.

ROWDY: I know someone who can take care of you –
someone better than your old man.

JOEY: Fuh yuh!

ROWDY: Unless you prefer him doing it!

JOEY: Nuh!

ROWDY: Your dad made you a world where you're
everything bud. I get that. But he's not well
enough to do that anymore and you're gonna
have to realize in everyone else's world you're not
everything.

JOEY: Ah kipah. (I'm crippled.)

ROWDY: And I'm brain damaged. No one cares. You wanna
live in this world then you gotta fight for it. No one's
parents hang around forever.

JOEY: Dah nuh gunuh dah. (Dad's not gonna die.)

ROWDY: You heard what the doc said. The pain's so bad they
have to drug him til it's like he's dead.

JOEY: Buh huh stuh uhluf. (But he's still alive.)

ROWDY: Not really.

PAUSE.

ROWDY: We can turn the lights out. She never has to see you.

JOEY: Huh wiw wuh puh huh? (How will we pay her?)

ROWDY: It's taken care of. You gotta do it Joe or we're both
gonna go crazy and start to hate each other.

JOEY: Yuh. Ukuh.

ROWDY: Great bud.

A LIGHT RISES ON JAKE IN HIS BED. ROBYN'S WITH HIM.

ROBYN: Glad to be home?

JAKE: Yeah. I can't go back there again. It was horrible.

ROBYN: Your sister's been very good about keeping me up to date.

JAKE: Good. I've held off taking my painkillers so we can talk.

ROBYN: Jake you shouldn't –

JAKE: If I don't I'm mostly incomprehensible but I'm not sure how long I can stand this.

ROBYN: I'm so so sorry.

JAKE: I don't deserve this.

ROBYN: No you don't.

JAKE: You don't have to worry about what'll happen to your sons if you're sick and disabled.

ROBYN: No.

JAKE: Your beautiful blessed family.

ROBYN: Well it isn't all sweetness and light but thank you.

JAKE: They're all well I hope.

ROBYN: Sure. Well the boys have some intimacy issues they blame on me but whatever. I kept meaning to come by.

JAKE: You don't need to lie to me Robyn.

ROBYN: I'm sorry. Your – the entire house kind of smells like pee and – something else.

JAKE: Despair. I know. *(THEY LAUGH.)* I always –

JAKE'S EYES GROW WIDE AND SIGHTLESS. HE HUMS QUIETLY.

ROBYN: Jake?

JAKE TWISTS HIS HEAD ODDLY AND MOANS.

ROBYN: Jake!

JAKE STOPS HUMMING AND STARES AT HER FOR A MOMENT.

ROBYN: It's me. Robyn.

        JAKE SHAKES HIS HEAD.

ROBYN: Remember?

JAKE: He makes you uncomfortable doesn't he?

ROBYN: Joey?

JAKE: Yes.

ROBYN: I'm just – Yes. A bit. I'm sorry.

JAKE: A lot of the problem with people like Joey is that they're not stimulated enough physically or mentally. They need so much attention and reinforcement –

ROBYN: Jake if you need money you know I can –

JAKE: I want to kill myself.

ROBYN: No.

JAKE: There's no cure. No real relief. I have every reason and right to take control of my pain and my life and end it and I don't give a flying fuck if some law based on someone's deranged religious beliefs says I can't.

ROBYN: Of course –

JAKE: Unfortunately the little insurance I have will disappear completely if I commit suicide. The only way I can continue to have the money to keep the house is by being alive.

ROBYN: That's not right.

JAKE: Say you'll visit him. Tuesday nights.

ROBYN: Visit him and do what?

JAKE: Talk to him. Play games. Whatever.

ROBYN: I can't believe you'd do this. We have an understanding.

JAKE: It should give you an idea of just how desperate I am.

ROBYN: Putting me on the spot like this.

JAKE: You're my only friend.

ROBYN: It's unfair.

PAUSE.

ROBYN: I don't even understand what he's saying.

JAKE: Everyone's like that in the beginning. We're so strained already Robyn. Just coming by for a few hours a week would give Rowdy a break and just – just – it would – mean –

JAKE'S EYES GROW WIDE. HE BEGINS TO HUM AGAIN.

ROBYN: Jake?

JAKE COMES AROUND.

JAKE: I have to take my painkillers now. My heart's beating too fast.

ROBYN: I should go anyway.

SHE KISSES HIM QUICKLY AND SQUEEZES HIS HAND.

JAKE: Night.

ROBYN: Good-bye.

ROBYN EXITS. JAKE TAKES HIS PILLS AND SOME WATER WITH GREAT EFFORT. HE LIES BACK, BREATHING HEAVILY. A LIGHT RISES ON ROWDY IN THE BATHROOM WITH JOEY WHO'S BEEN BATHED AND IS NOW BEING SHAVED. HE WEARS A BATHROBE AND SWEATS.

ROWDY: Hold still.

JOEY: Kuhfuh. (Careful.)

ROWDY: Shut up or I'll cut you.

ROWDY SHAVES THE LAST OF THE FOAM FROM JOEY'S FACE. HE WIPES HIM CLEAN WITH A TOWEL.

ROWDY: A shave like that says I took the time.

JOEY: Duh Ah luh ukuh? (Do I look okay.)

ROWDY: Never looked better. First blow job. This is a very exciting time in any guy's life. Usually it happens with drunk girls in cars but whatever works right?

JOEY: Duh wuh ah tisetud wuh fleeh huh owd? (The way I'm twisted won't freak her out?)

ROWDY: She's done way worse bro. I explained that to you. This is how she gives back.

ROWDY WHEELS JOEY INTO THE KITCHEN AS THEY SPEAK.

JOEY: Huh luh? (How long?)

ROWDY: We've got a few minutes yet.

JOEY: Dah wuh kuh owd? (Dad won't come out?)

ROWDY: He took his meds about an hour ago.

PAUSE.

JOEY: Wowdee –

ROWDY: Yeah.

JOEY: Duh shus aw huh buh ah wush. (The sores on his back are worse.)

ROWDY: I know. We keep shifting him like they tell us but it doesn't seem to help.

JOEY: Uh luh hesh uh towshuh yuh ulh. (It's like he's a thousand years old.)

ROWDY: Put it outa your head for the next hour for sure bud.

JOEY: Ah nuvush. (I'm nervous.)

ROWDY: Just relax and let her do her thing. It'll come natural.

JOEY: Ruh. (Right.)

ROWDY: And I guarantee you this will make you a lot less angry all the time.

JOEY: Muh frunsh un duh nud suh owah sush ish ukuh wuhow uh cuduh. (My friends on the net say oral sex is okay without a condom.)

ROWDY: Sure long as she doesn't have the herpes or a syph sore in her mouth which I'm pretty sure she doesn't. You'll love it. Trust me.

THE DOORBELL RINGS.

JOEY: Uhuh. (Ohoh.)

ROWDY: Quick go into your bedroom.

JOEY: Ahl tun duh luh owd. (I'll turn the light out.)

ROWDY: Whatever you need to do Joe.

JOEY EXITS. THE DOORBELL RINGS AGAIN. LIGHTS RISE ON JAKE'S BEDROOM. HE IS SLEEPING HEAVILY. TWYLA IS DUSTING, SINGING QUIETLY. JAKE WAKES.

JAKE: Viola?

TWYLA: It's me.

JAKE: Shorry. I've been sleeping too much.

TWYLA: How's the pain?

JAKE: I'm okay.

TWYLA: It's nice to see you up.

JAKE: How are you?

TWYLA: Alright. I – there was an incident –

JAKE: Incident?

TWYLA: A few days ago. Joey walked in while – uh – while Rowdy and I were –

JAKE: What?

TWYLA: Kissing. It seemed to upset him.

JAKE: You're his two best friends. Of course it upset him.

TWYLA: I've tried to talk to him but he hasn't been very – open.

JAKE: I think the real issue here might be why were you being intimate with Rowdy?

TWYLA: It was a – vulnerable moment and he was being – surprisingly charming. Are you hungry?

JAKE: No.

TWYLA: One other thing.

JAKE: What?

TWYLA: The Service's pay for a certain – understanding woman to visit Joey once a month.

JAKE: Wow. He said he didn't want that.

TWYLE: Rowdy changed his mind.

JAKE: Does it – help?

TWYLA: It really does.

JAKE: Then.

TWYLA: Exactly.

JAKE: And you?

TWYLA: Fine.

JAKE: Fine?

TWYLA: For someone with no life.

JAKE: I know we ask a lot of you –

TWYLA: I can't – can't keep doing this.

JAKE: You have to.

TWYLA: I'm so fucking tired. Running around – paying bills – juggling work – worrying –

JAKE: He doesn't have anyone else!

TWYLA: Stop being sick! You wrote a novel while you were working as a waiter. You kept me going after our mom and Viola died. I know how strong you are –

JAKE: You think I want to be like this?

TWYLA: I can't deal with this alone!

JAKE: What the fuck am I supposed to say? There's nothing I can do.

TWYLA: I know.

JAKE: Then stop being mad at me.

TWYLA: I try not to be.

JAKE: I raised you after the accident –

TWYLA: And I've been Joey's mother –

JAKE: So it's a contest now?

TWYLA: I didn't say that –

JAKE MOANS.

TWYLA: Jake?

JAKE: It's okay.

TWYLA: You need your drugs.

JAKE: Joey's computer alarm should bring him any time.

TWYLA: I'm sorry. That was wrong. I know you can't do more than you are.

JAKE: I understand your fr – *(MOANS.)* frustration.

TWYLA: Where's Joey?

JAKE: I'm okay.

TWYLA: I'll get him.

JAKE: Don't worry.

JOEY ENTERS.

TWYLA: Where have you been?

JAKE: I really need my meds.

JOEY: Nuh yeh. (Not yet.)

TWYLA: Why not?

JOEY: Wuh nud tuh tak. (We need to talk.)

TWYLA: About what?

JOEY: Oofunushuh.

JAKE: What?

JOEY: Oofunushuh.

TWYLA: Sorry?

JOEY PRESSES A BUTTON ON HIS TABLET. A BOOMING VOICE IS HEARD.

VOICE: Euthanasia. The act of assisting in the death of another person when it is the only way to save them from pain and suffering. Sometimes known as mercy killing –

TWYLA: Joey!

JAKE: Turn it off.

JOEY STOPS THE VOICE. PAUSE.

TWYLA: Euthanasia?

JOEY: Ah bulun tuh uh goob un duh pooduh dah desw wuf duh rust uv dushubuh pupuh. Wuh nuh tuh dikush oofunushuh. (I belong to a group on the computer that deals with the rights of disabled people. We need to discuss euthanasia.)

JAKE: Why?

JOEY: Bukush ah duh wah yuh tuh twuh tuh kih muh wuh yuh kund tuk cuh fuh muh unuhmuh. (Because I don't want you to try to kill me when you can't take care of me anymore.)

TWYLA: Joey?

JOEY: Pupuh duh ud aw duh tum ih thuh sushiashuh. Day fing ih wiw buh buduh fuh ufuhweh. (People do it all the time in this situation. They think it will be better for everyone.)

JAKE: Son you know –

JOEY: Duh tuh muh yuh huvuh toth ubuh ih. (Don't tell me you haven't thought about it.)

JAKE: I can't stand the thought of you being alone –

JOEY: Ah wun buh uhluh. Un ah dun wunuh dah. Pumush. (I won't be alone. And I don't wanna die. Promise.)

PAUSE.

JAKE: Okay I promise. No murder suicide.

JOEY: Um nuh jukuh. (I'm not joking.)

JAKE: Neither am I. *(JAKE STIFLES A MOAN.)* But maybe we should talk about that medication now.

JOEY: Un dah.

JAKE: What?

JOEY: Ah nuh huh muh pah yuh ah ih. Ih wung fuh yuh tuh buh leg tish. (I know how much pain you are in. It's wrong for you to be like this.)

JAKE: I don't have a lot of other options.

JOEY: Yuh. Yuh duh. Un al duh uh. Ah duh cuh abuh duh nushewanch. (Yes. You do. And I'll do it. I don't care about the insurance.)

TWYLA: Joey stop –

JAKE: Okay thank you for the discussion. Can I have my pill now? Please.

JOEY PUSHES THE PILL CONTAINER ON HIS CHAIR TRAY TOWARD HIS FATHER.

TWYLA: Let me.

TWYLA GETS THE PILL AND HANDS IT TO JAKE.

JAKE: Thank you Joey for bringing this up. That tablet was quite the gift.

JAKE TAKES HIS PILL.

JOEY: Yuh. Ah luh tuh tuk tuh pupuh. Ah juh wus ah cuh tup buduh. (Yeah. I like to talk to people. I just wish I could type better.)

TWYLA: You do just fine.

JOEY: Thush muh buduh shuv dah Muguh Wums ad puhn. (There's much better stuff than Magic Worms and porn.)

JAKE: You're shush a good boy.

JOEY: Yuh huh. (You're high.)

JAKE: Promish me shumthing.

TWYLA: What?

JAKE: Whudevuh happensh. I dunt want to go bag to the hoshpital. I don't want to be in pain.

JOEY: Uh kush.

TWYLA: If that's what you want.

JAKE MOANS SOFTLY SINKING BACK INTO THE BED.

JOEY: Ah hah huhwuk tuh duh. (I have homework to do.)

JAKE: Homework?

JOEY: Yeah.

JAKE AND TWYLA SHARE A LOOK.

JAKE: Goonight shun.

JOEY: Nah Dah.

TWYLA: Sleep well.

JAKE: Uh wiw.

JAKE FALLS ASLEEP, BREATHING HEAVILY. JOEY AND TWYLA WATCH HIM FOR A MOMENT, UNTIL THEY'RE SURE HE'S OUT.

TWYLA: Joey I don't know if this was the right time to bring all of that up.

JOEY: Uh huh duh. Wuy huh stih ubuh tuh thuk. (I had to. While he's still able to think.)

TWYLA: I don't believe in heaven and all that stuff. Who could in this family right? But I think like – you know – we don't know everything even though we think we do. And we really don't know what happens after we die. Maybe it all is just over but maybe – you know like – we become something else. We're transformed into – energy or another state or – something else – some completely natural biological process we can't understand any more than the caterpillar can understand it's gonna someday be a butterfly or a tadpole knows it's gonna be a frog. And maybe that thing we turn into is a really really great thing and it makes all of this shit happening now completely meaningless. But what happens if you don't die the way you're supposed to? What if interfering with that natural process somehow stops you from – achieving that next state and you really do just end in nothing when there's a chance something else might've happened? He's my big brother. I have to keep hoping –

JOEY: Uh nuh. Bud id dash luf. Id dunuh maduh wuh yuh thung. (I know. But it's dad's life. It doesn't matter what you think.)

TWYLA: But he has times when he's almost completely normal.

JOEY: Nuh suh mh unuhmuh. (Not so much anymore.)

TWYLA: Things can change so fast –

JOEY: Eshagluh. Fuh buduh uh wush. Wuh hud duh nuh wuh huh wundsh. (Exactly. For better or worse. We had to know what he wants.)

TWYLA: It was the drugs.

JOEY: Ih wuh thuh pun. (It was the pain.)

PAUSE.

JOEY: Un Un tuluh. (And Aunt Twyla.)

TWYLA: What?

JOEY: Uh dun thung yuh shuh dwing und dwuf unuhmuh. (I don't think you should drink and drive anymore.)

TWYLA: Joey –

JOEY: Wuh thuh unluh wus lufd. (We're the only ones left.)

PAUSE.

TWYLA: Come on. It's time for bed.

LIGHTS RISE ON THE KITCHEN WHERE ROWDY IS GOING THROUGH THE FRIDGE CHECKING THE EXPIRY DATES ON THE FOOD, AND TOSSING OLD STUFF OUT, MUTTERING TO HIMSELF.

ROWDY: Good. Good. Old. Good. Good. Good. *(TASTES SOMETHING.)* Old. Old. Good.

THERE'S A KNOCK AT THE DOOR. ROWDY HOLLERS WITHOUT INTERRUPTING HIS WORK.

ROWDY: It's open. Good. Old. Good.

ROBYN ENTERS.

ROBYN: Hello.

ROWDY: Well aren't you a sight for sore eyes?

ROBYN: Robyn –

ROWDY: Yeah yeah. The married lady who loves Mr Sturdy.

ROBYN: Who told you that?

ROWDY: You did.

ROBYN: I certainly did not.

ROWDY: Well not with words but we all saw the way you looked at him. Also saw your wedding ring. Oh wait that's not the kind of thing I'm supposed to say out loud is it?

ROBYN: No it's not.

ROWDY CLOSES THE FRIDGE AND TIES UP THE TRASH BAG.

ROWDY: Mr S took his pills about an hour ago so he's out like a light.

ROBYN: Don't worry. I'm not here –

JOEY ENTERS.

JOEY: Huh. (Hey.)

ROBYN: Hello Joey. How are you?

JOEY: Wuh cuh wuh dah ub. (We can't wake dad up.)

ROWDY: He says we can't wake his dad up.

ROBYN: After Jake was in the hospital last time he asked me if I'd drop by and – you know – hang out on Tuesday nights.

JOEY: Wuh?

ROBYN: He said he thought everyone would like an evening off.

ROWDY: That is so amazing! I can't tell you how amazing that is! I really need a night off. No offense Joe but I gotta get out of here.

JOEY: Shuh.

ROWDY: Mam you are so damn excellent! I'm gonna grab a quick shower shave and shit – pardon my French – and get outa here and do some moon howling!

ROWDY EXITS.

ROBYN: He's very – enthusiastic.

JOEY: Tuh muh ubuh ih. (Tell me about it.)

ROBYN: How bad is it with Jake?

JOEY: Sumtuh guh sumtuh buh. (Sometimes good
          sometimes bad.)

ROBYN: I'm sorry.

JOEY: Ih nuh yuh fuwd. (It's not your fault.)

ROBYN: I mean for not coming back. When you asked me
          to.

          JOEY SHRUGS.

ROBYN: It was very hard for me to see your father like this
          and honestly Joey you frightened me a bit.

JOEY: Wuh?

ROBYN: Because I've never known anyone like you.

JOEY: Ah nuh uh munshuh. (I'm not a monster.)

ROBYN: Did you say I'm not a monster?

JOEY: Yuh.

ROBYN: I never thought you were. But I was concerned you
          might think I'm stupid if I couldn't understand you
          as well as everybody else does.

JOEY: Ih tush suh tum. (It takes some time.)

ROBYN: Time right?

JOEY: Yuh.

ROBYN: Okay. So what would you normally do tonight?

JOEY: Wush suh shoopuh tuhvuh wiv Wowdee uh pluh uh
          my pootah. (Watch some stupid TV with Rowdy or
          play on my computer.)

ROBYN: I got watch TV play on computer.

JOEY: Yuh. Wuh wooh ooh nuhmuhluh duh? (Yes. What
          would you normally do.)

ROBYN: Well normally I'd see your father and we'd –

JOEY: Pluh hukuh? (Play hockey?)

JOEY LAUGHS.

ROBYN: Are you trying to embarrass me?

JOEY: Nuh. Yuh wuh pudeyuh thah uh hukuh gum. (No. You're way prettier than a hockey game.)

ROBYN: Flatterer.

JOEY: Wowdee shez wuhmuh unuhstuh flutureh ih unuh lunwish. (Rowdy says women understand flattery in any language.)

ROBYN: Sorry. That was a bit too complicated.

JOEY: Yuh smuh nush. (You smell nice.)

ROBYN: Thank you.

ROWDY ENTERS, CLEANED UP.

ROWDY: Aren't I a spifter? Check it out.

ROBYN: I have to go at ten thirty.

ROWDY: I will return at that hour.

JOEY: Yuh buduh. (You better.)

ROWDY: And just so you know mam – we don't judge people here.

ROBYN: Judge people?

ROWDY: No one's gonna ask about your husband.

ROWDY EXITS. PAUSE.

JOEY: Ah gush wuhl wash tuhvuh. (I guess we'll watch TV.)

ROBYN: I did bring a book –

JOEY: *(BORED ALREADY.)* Uh bug?

ROBYN TAKES THE BOOK FROM HER PURSE.

ROBYN: Yes. I realize it's not a computer game or whatever
          but I think you might be a little bit interested since
          your father wrote it.

JOEY: Muh dah?

ROBYN: Yes.

          *ROBYN SETS THE BOOK ON THE TRAY OF HIS CHAIR.
          JOEY TOUCHES IT.*

JOEY: Rod uh bug? (Wrote a book?)

ROBYN: It was published when you were just a baby.
          It's dedicated to you –

JOEY: Muh?

ROBYN: And your mother.

JOEY: Muh muhmuh?

ROBYN: Yes. He never told you about it?

JOEY: Nuh. Nufuh. (No. Never.)

          PAUSE.

JOEY: Ush ih uh guh bug? (Is it a good book?)

ROBYN: Yes it is.

          (JOEY READS THE TITLE.)

JOEY: Wivuh Wuh Wapuh?

ROBYN: I thought I could read you a few chapters when we
          get together. Would you like that?

JOEY: *(SHOCKED.)* Yuh. Uh wud.

ROBYN: Then that's what we'll do.

          LIGHTS RISE ON ROWDY AND TWYLA IN THE PARK.

TWYLA: Thank you for waiting outside. They get really
          uptight about personal interaction at work.

ROWDY: I didn't want to seem stalkery it's just that I know
          you've been like avoiding me ever since that time –

TWYLA: It just got me a bit confused.

ROWDY: I'm a people pleaser. And all you do is take care of people –

TWYLA: I don't just take care of people –

ROWDY: I'm just sayin' you don't have a lot of people in your life who look out for you.

TWYLA: If you think this is going anywhere –

ROWDY: Going anywhere?

TWYLA: Romantic.

ROWDY: Me?

TWYLA: Yeah.

ROWDY: No no no. You're the one who's falling in love with me.

TWYLA: What?

ROWDY: That's why you're uncomfortable.

TWYLA: I'm uncomfortable because I don't want to do anything that can be construed as leading you on.

ROWDY: I'm a bad bet for romance.

TWYLA: Then let's not have a romance.

ROWDY: Sure.

TWYLA: Even if it were a possibility the situation is totally inappropriate –

ROWDY: Yeah cuz there's nothing inappropriate going on in either of our worlds.

TWYLA: That's sharkism right?

ROWDY: Yeah. But y'know –

TWYLA: What?

ROWDY: You're probably not going to meet a lot of guys who want to make sure you feel good over the next little while.

TWYLA: So?

ROWDY: If I know there's no possibility of romance I don't really care what you think of me so I'm not afraid to be a total fucking pig.

TWYLA: That was really – not romantic.

ROWDY: See – nuthin' to be afraid of.

TWYLA: When would we find all this time to be – not romantic?

ROWDY: Well the adulterous lady sez she wantsa spend Tuesday night's with Joey so I'm figuring –

TWYLA: I do have a place.

ROWDY: Maybe you could take me there now so I can find it next Tuesday.

TWYLA: No one can ever know.

ROWDY: It's just a couple hours of nothing but us.

TWYLA: And if either of us meets someone else?

ROWDY: We see what happens. Wait.

TWYLA: What?

ROWDY: Just so I don't feel like a total whore.

ROWDY KISSES HER GENTLY.

TWYLA: I really shouldn't –

ROWDY: Yeah I know. But mildly retarded and well hung. Not many can resist.

LIGHTS RISE ON THE KITCHEN. JAKE SITS AT THE TABLE WRITING FEVERISHLY BY HAND IN A NOTEPAD, DRINKING A GLASS OF RYE. HE LAUGHS QUIETLY AND MUTTERS TO HIMSELF.

JAKE: The father's story – and the son. Broken son. Dead mother. Sad – not sad – tired sister. Sad house. Pain. But funny. Funny. Dark funny.

ROWDY ENTERS.

ROWDY: Mr S?

JAKE: Wry observances.

ROWDY: Mr Sturdy?

JAKE: Just getting in?

ROWDY: Yeah. What's going on?

JAKE: Writing.

ROWDY: It's not your usual pill time.

JAKE: I woke up and just got this urge to write. I don't know why. I haven't written anything in years.

ROWDY: Do you need a pill?

JAKE: Had some rye. Seems to be working.

ROWDY: Where's Joey?

JAKE: Sleeping.

JAKE WAVES THE BOTTLE AT ROWDY. ROWDY GETS A GLASS.

ROWDY: Sure.

JAKE: Last one.

JAKES POURS THEM DRINKS.

ROWDY: Why you writing?

JAKE: I'm a writer.

ROWDY: You're a teacher.

JAKE: Before that. I wrote a novel. It was very promising. Sold some copies.

ROWDY: Joey never told me.

JAKE: He doesn't know.

ROWDY: Why not?

JAKE: I don't know – I just – after his mother died and it was just me and him and Twyla – my imagination – changed. I don't know how to explain it. It was like – like the only thing I could imagine anymore was his future and it was just too fucking hard and sad and –

PAUSE.

ROWDY: What did you write?

JAKE: Want to read it?

ROWDY: Your pages?

JAKE: If you had a minute.

ROWDY: You could read it to me.

JAKE: Yeah?

ROWDY: Sure. I read real slow.

JAKE: You don't mind?

ROWDY: I'm here to keep the Sturdys happy. Go.

PAUSE.

ROWDY: Whenever.

PAUSE.

ROWDY: Mr S?

JAKE: Never mind.

ROWDY: What's wrong?

JAKE: I can't read my fucking handwriting.

ROWDY: What?

JAKE: It's just scribbles.

ROWDY: Let's see.

JAKE HANDS ROWDY THE PAPERS. ROWDY EXAMINES THEM.

ROWDY: Scribbles.

JAKE: I wrote it. I sat here and I –

PAUSE.

JAKE: I wrote it.

ROWDY: It's okay.

PAUSE. JAKE DOWNS HIS DRINK, GRABS HIS CANE AND STANDS.

JAKE: I could use that pill now. We don't need to – tell anyone else about this right?

ROWDY: Right.

JAKE: Thanks Rowdy.

ROWDY: No prob.

JAKE EXITS. ROWDY FINISHES HIS DRINK THEN TAKES THE PAGES AND RIPS THEM INTO SMALL PIECES. HE THROWS THE PAPER BITS INTO THE GARBAGE CAN AND EXITS AS A LIGHT RISES ON ROBYN ALONE ON HER COMMUNICATIONS DEVICE.

ROBYN: Joey I just got your text. You haven't given me a lot of notice but I think I can do some rearranging and make it. If you're sure you want me there. I mean I want to come. I'll do my best. And thank you.

LIGHTS RISE ON JAKE'S BEDROOM. JOEY IS WEARING A SUIT AND LOOKS VERY CLEANED UP. HE'S SHAKING HIS FATHER, WHO'S SOUND ASLEEP IN HIS BED.

JOEY: Dah. Wug ub. (Dad. Wake Up.)

JAKE MOANS BUT DOESN'T WAKE.

JOEY: Wuh huf tuh guh tuh thuh shooh. (We have to go to the school.)

JAKE MUMBLES UNINTELLIGABLEY. JOEY SHAKES HIM.

JOEY: Uhn guduahshuh duduh. (I'm graduating today.)

JAKE: Guduahshuh?

JOEY: Yuh.

JAKE: Yuh guduashuh from – school?

JOEY: Yuh!

JAKE: Duday?

JOEY: Yuh dah.

JAKE: I wunuh mish id.

TWYLA ENTERS CARRYING A BASIN OF WATER.

TWYLA: He's awake.

JOEY: Shordah. (Sorta.)

TWYLA: We're just gonna clean you up a bit.

TWYLA SETS THE BASIN DOWN AND SOAKS A WASHCLOTH IN IT.

JAKE: Wun did I lasht shower?

JOEY: Ush buh uh fuh dush. (It's been a few days.)

JAKE: Ah should showuh.

TWYLA REMOVES HIS PAJAMA TOP.

TWYLA: It'll be a sponge bath today bro. We don't have much time.

JAKE: Whah about muh hair?

TWYLA: We'll get you all fixed up.

TWYLA WASHES JAKE AS THEY SPEAK.

JOEY: Ah funust shooh dah. (I finished school dad.)

TWYLA: His marks are really good.

JAKE: Thash suh great.

JOEY: Huh munuh push dud yuh tuk? (How many pills did you take?)

JAKE: Fuh.

TWYLA: Four?

JAKE: Ah fun.

TWYLA: Keep telling yourself that until the graduation's over.

JAKE: Don scrub suh hard!

TWYLA: I'm not.

ROWDY ENTERS.

ROWDY: What can I do?

TWYLA: Got his clothes.

ROWDY: Yeah.

ROWDY: You okay Mr S?

JAKE: Tiud and dishy bud fun.

ROWDY: Not so clear there.

JOEY: Tiud un dishy bud fun. (Tired and dizzy but fine.)

ROWDY: How much does it hurt to move around?

JAKE: Lotsh und lotsh.

TWYLA: Do you think he needs a shave?

ROWDY: We don't have a lot of time.

JOEY: Nuh uh publuh. (Not a problem.)

TWYLA: Let's get him into that suit.

THEY DRESS JAKE AS THE SCENE PROGRESSES.

ROWDY: Give me a hand so I can get the pants on.

TWYLA: I've got him.

ROWDY: One leg at a time. Nice and easy.

JAKE GROANS AS HE GETS INTO THE PANTS.

TWYLA: I'll hold you steady.

ROWDY: Just keep him up until I get him zipped.

JOEY: Yuh Ukuh dah? (You okay dad?)

JAKE: Ish okay. Uhm feeluh a bit shtronguh. Uh couldn't mish thish.

TWYLA: Hold your arms out so Rowdy can put the shirt on.

JAKE: Wud wuh we do wivout Rowdy?

ROWDY: Nuthin I'll tell you that.

TWYLA: The van's waiting.

ROWDY: You look very nice Twyla.

TWYLA: So do you Rowdy.

JOEY: Wuh ubuh muh? (What about me?)

TWYLA GOES TO JOEY AND KISSES HIM ON THE FOREHEAD.

TWYLA: You look great. And all grown up.

JAKE: When – when dih thah happen?

TWYLA: It's always happening.

ROWDY: Okay so really I have no idea how to tie a tie.

TWYLA: Oh dear.

JOEY: Dun looh ah muh. (Don't look at me.)

JAKE: Muh hands cand quite munug.

ROBYN ENTERS.

ROBYN: You know I'm actually quite good with ties.

JOEY: Wubuh. (Robyn.)

ROBYN: The front door was wide open.

JAKE: Robyn?

JOEY: See buh spunduh Tushduh nush wiv muh. (She's been spending Tuesday nights with me.)

ROWDY: Thank god.

JAKE: For how luh?

ROBYN: You haven't told him?

JOEY: Nuh yuh. (Not yet.)

TWYLA: Told him what?

JOEY: Wubuh uh ah wed yuh bug? (Robyn and I read your book.)

JAKE: Muh bug?

ROBYN: The whole thing.

JAKE: Yuh – yuh liged it?

JOEY: Yuh. Ooh uh vuwuh gud widuh. (You're a very good writer.)

JAKE: Uh cand tell you how mush that meansh tuh muh.

JOEY: – Seesh uh weewee gwud laduh. (She's a really great lady.)

JAKE OPENS HIS ARMS AND WALKS TOWARD JOEY STIFFLY, AS IF TO EMBRACE HIM.

JAKE: Uh am suh proud of my boy –

THERE'S A RUDE NOISE. EVERYONE FREEZES.

JOEY: Dah?

ROWDY: Peeyou.

JAKE: I jusht shat my pantsh didun I?

TWYLA: It's okay.

JAKE: I cun few it running dun thu bug of muh legsh.

ROBYN: Just an accident.

JAKE: Fuck.

JOEY: Ih ukuh. (It's okay.)

JAKE: FUCK!

ROBYN: Don't.

JAKE FALLS TO HIS KNEES. HIS EYES ROLL BACK IN HIS HEAD.

JOEY: Dah!

JAKE MAKES A STRANGE MOANING SOUND.

ROWDY: Ah hell.

TWYLA: Watch his head.

ROWDY: Got him

JAKE CONVULSES IN ROWDY'S ARMS.

ROBYN: Jake? Can you hear me?

JAKE HUMS THEN GROWS STILL.

JOEY: Guh ub dah. (Get up dad.)

ROWDY: Mr S.

JOEY: Geh ub. Geh duh fuh ub! Dah! Geh ub! Preesh dah. Geh ub. (Get up. Get the fuck up! Dad! Get up! Please dad. Get up.)

TWYLA: We should call an ambulance.

JOEY: Nuh!

TWYLA: No really –

JOEY: Nuh umbulast. Hew geh ub. Dah. (No ambulance. He'll get up. Dad.)

ROWDY: He's not getting up.

TWYLA: The ambulance –

JOEY: Nuh! Kun hum ub un puh hum bag du bud. (No! Clean him up and put him back to bed.)

ROWDY: You sure?

JOEY: Yuh.

ROBYN: Your graduation –

JOEY: Dun muduh. (Doesn't matter.)

TWYLA: His doctors need to know it's gotten worse.

JOEY: Wuh?! Thuh cand duh unuthuh abuh ih! (Why? They can't do anything about it.)

TWYLA: He's still alive!

JOEY: Thash nuh lubuh! (That's not living.)

TWYLA: We cannot have this conversation.

JOEY: Wuh huf tuh. (We have to.)

ROBYN: I'm afraid he's right.

TWYLA: But the hospital can make him comfortable and The Services will send more people –

JOEY: Hush nuh gouh tun unuh husputuh. (He's not going to any hospital.)

TWYLA: Maybe we should talk to Jake – after he wakes up. We'll see what he wants.

JOEY: Ah nuh whuh huh wunsh. Und sho duh yuh. Huh toad ush. (I know what he wants. And so do you. He told us.)

TWYLA: I know but –

JOEY: Nuh tuh buh ah thuh hopsitah. Nuh tuh buh ih pen. (Not to be back at the hospital. Not to be in pain.)

ROWDY: Didn't the doc say shitting his pants was the worst sign? He'd be like totally fucked up?

JOEY: Yuh.

PAUSE.

TWYLA: Joey we can't –

JOEY: Huh shah huh. (He stays here.)

JAKE WAKES AND TRIES TO SIT UP.

JAKE: Shorry. We can still make it ruh? Joey ish nut tuh late?

JOEY: Ih ukuh dah. (It's okay dad.)

JAKE: Muh legsh few funny.

ROBYN TAKES JAKE IN HER ARMS.

ROBYN: It's okay Jake.

JAKE: Shun I'm suruh.

JOEY: Duh shwuh ih. (Don't sweat it.)

ROBYN: We're all right here.

JAKE: Ah shtink.

ROBYN: We're going to clean you up.

JAKE: Uhm mishing id ah. Everuhshing.

ROBYN: It's okay.

JAKE BEGINS SOBBING HYSTERICALLY. ROBYN COMFORTS HIM.

JAKE: Ish not fuh. Ish not fuging fuh! Shun ah sho shorry.

ROBYN: It's okay. Cry all you want.

JOEY: Wuh shuh kuh yuh ub dah. (We should clean you up dad.)

ROWDY: I'll do it.

TWYLA: We can –

ROWDY: It's okay. I've done it before. Come on Mr S.

ROWDY AND ROBYN HELP JAKE UP.

TWYLA: It's gonna be okay.

JAKE: No.

TWYLA: I know.

TWYLA HUGS HIM.

TWYLA: I love you Jake.

JAKE: Uh love yuh too.

ROBYN: You don't have to worry about anything.

JAKE: Nuh?

ROBYN: Absolutely not.

JAKE: Thung yuh.

ROBYN KISSES JAKE.

ROWDY: Come on now.

ROWDY LEADS JAKE OUT OF THE ROOM. PAUSE.

ROBYN: We'll wait here.

JOEY: Ahl caw ooh tumuruh – (I'll call you tomorrow –)

TWYLA: No. We're staying here.

ROBYN: Right here.

JOEY: Buh iv thuh fun owd – (But if they find out –)

TWYLA: We're staying.

PAUSE. JOEY NODS.

JOEY: Ah huv tuh gud sumthug. (I have to get something.)

JOEY EXITS TO JAKE'S ROOM. TWYLA AND ROBYN SHARE A LOOK.

ROBYN: Jesus.

TWYLA: This isn't really happening.

ROBYN: It is.

PAUSE.

TWYLA: Drink.

ROBYN: Definitely.

TWYLA POURS THEM TWO VERY LARGE DRINKS. LIGHTS RISE IN THE BATHROOM. JAKE IS IN THE TUB.

ROWDY: This isn't hurting you is it?

JAKE: I – I dunno. Muh body feelsh different.

ROWDY: I think we shoulda called that ambulance.

JAKE: Nuh.

ROWDY: You sure?

JAKE: Yuh.

JOEY ENTERS.

JOEY: Huh ih huh? (How is he?)

ROWDY: A little better.

JOEY: Wuwuh wum enuh? (Water warm enough?)

JAKE: It is.

JOEY: Yuh wunuh drung dah? (You want a drink dad?)

JAKE: That would be so nice.

JOEY: Wowdee geh dash susuh un uh glush. (Rowdy get dad's CC and a glass.)

ROWDY: You alright in there Mister Sturdy?

JAKE: Ahl buh fun.

ROWDY: Back in a flash.

JOEY: Sanks.

ROWDY EXITS. JOEY WHEELS HIS CHAIR CLOSER TO THE TUB, SPEAKING URGENTLY.

JAKE: I'm sho shorry shon –

JOEY: Duh suh duh. (Don't say that.)

JAKE: Uh keep letting you dun.

JOEY: Ih nud yuh foud. (It's not your fault.)

JAKE: Joey –

JOEY: Wowdee un Un Tuhluh un Wubuh wiw tuh gud kuh uh muh. (Rowdy and Aunt Twyla and Robyn will take good care of me.)

JAKE: Thuh unshrance – ?

JOEY: Ahl suh duh hush un wuh wiw guh uh aputmuh. (I'll sell the house and we'll get an apartment.)

ROWDY ENTERS WITH THE RYE WHICH HE SETS ON THE SIDE OF THE TUB WITH A GLASS.

ROWDY: The rye.

JAKE: Rowdy?

JOEY: Yuh ukuh?

ROWDY POURS JAKE A BIG GLASS OF RYE.

ROWDY: I know what's going on alright? I know what you're planning and I know why and I just fucking hate it. I hate it. But I love you both so I'm thinking I should do it – right? It makes sense. I've already got a record. Whatever you need. Poison neck breaking throat slitting – it's all gross but I'd do it for you guys. I would –

JOEY: Nuh.

ROWDY: Why not?

JOEY: Hesh muh dah.

ROWDY: You can still get into trouble –

JOEY: Ah duh cuh!

ROWDY: Sure.

ROWDY: You were like the father I never had sir.

JAKES SHAKES ROWDY'S HAND.

JAKE: Tag gud cah of hum.

ROWDY MOVES TO JOEY, HUGS HIM FEROCIOUSLY.

ROWDY: You know where I'll be.

ROWDY EXITS FAST. JOEY PUSHES THE PILL CONTAINER ON HIS TRAY TOWARD JAKE WHO PICKS IT UP AND SETS IT ON THE SIDE OF THE TUB NEXT TO THE RYE.

JAKE: Pillsh booze und ah fuh tub. Shounds like uh reshipuh fuh dishastuh.

JOEY: *(LAUGHS NERVOUSLY.)* Yuh.

JAKE: Uh couldun have asht fuh a bedduh shun.

JOEY: Uh skud dah. (I'm scared dad.)

JAKE: Muh tuh.

PAUSE.

JAKE: Yuh shud prubuluh guh nuh.

JOEY: Guh?

JAKE: Yuh.

JOEY: Nuh.

JAKE: Yuh dun wanna be huh.

JOEY: Ah duh.

JAKE: Shun nuh –

JOEY: Ah wuh tuh buh wiv ooh tih duh vewuh und.

*JOEY TOUCHES HIS FATHER WITH ONE OF HIS HANDS.
JAKE LAYS HIS HAND OVER HIS SON'S.*

JAKE: Yuh shuh?

JOEY: Uf kush. Yuh mah dah.

FADE TO BLACK.

9 781783 198092